W9-BUE-476

THE ELEPHANT IN THE CHURCH

THE ELEPHANT IN THE CHURCH

WHAT YOU DON'T SEE CAN KILL YOUR MINISTRY

Jeanne Stevenson-Moessner
Mary Lynn Dell

Abingdon Press
Nashville

THE ELEPHANT IN THE CHURCH
WHAT YOU DON'T SEE CAN KILL YOUR MINISTRY

Copyright © 2013 by Abingdon Press

This book is printed on acid-free paper.

Library of Congress Cataloging-in-Publication Data has been requested

ISBN 978-1-4267-5321-3

All names and references are used as illustrations only and are drawn from multiple cases. All names are fictional, and any resemblance to actual persons is strictly coincidental.

13 14 15 16 17 18 19 20 21—10 9 8 7 6 5 4 3 2 1

MANUFACTURED IN THE UNITED STATES OF AMERICA

To Mary M. Davis

Whose courage and faith

have shown me how to journey through the jungle

—J.S.M.

To the Rev. Dr. Ronald Ricketts

Pastor, Theologian, Role Model, and

Indiana's Best Church Camper

—M.L.D.

CONTENTS

ACKNOWLEDGMENTS

It takes manifold survival skills to survive a jungle. I have dedicated this book to Mary Davis, teacher, mentor, and friend who is now 102 years of age. I was a teacher at St. Mary's Episcopal School in Memphis, Tennessee, when she was Dean in the early 1970s. She courageously stood with Head of School Nat Hughes to allow persons of all colors to be admitted. St. Mary's was the first private school in Memphis to do so; this action was placed before the Supreme Court's ruling. Board of Trustees members resigned, parents transferred children out of the school, but Mary Davis stood firm in her advocacy for all children. This tenacity of spirit had allowed her to survive many years earlier as a young widow with three girls. When I interviewed her recently, she recounted her early years in Nodoa, Hainan Province, China, as the daughter of Presbyterian missionaries. The mission compound was near the mountains where there were bandits, bandits who picked up children, picked up animals, to take back to their places in the mountains where they lived. Mary Davis learned from an early age the skills of survival, and I am extremely fortunate to continue to learn from her.

Acknowledgments

Without the persistence of Kathy Armistead at Abingdon Press, this book would not have emerged. Thank you to Kathy for her foresight and her determination to have a book on elephants in the church. Thank you also to Jennifer Manley Rogers, Abingdon production editor, who guided this book through the production process.

I have never journeyed alone. Thank you to my colleagues at Perkins School of Theology, Southern Methodist University, in Dallas. You colleagues have sharpened my theological perceptions through dialogue and difference. Thank you, Bill Lawrence, for your enthusiasm for this book. Thank you, Diana Coon and Carolyn Douglas, for your practical assistance in my work at Perkins. I am grateful for the support of the Office of Research and Graduate Studies at SMU, in particular to James Quick and Kathleen Hughley-Cook.

My friends in Dubuque, Iowa, in Memphis, Tennessee, and in Lake Cormorant, Mississippi, have been faithful travelling companions. Dr. Roberta Berger has counseled me at many forks in the road. I am delighted that Mary Lynn Dell and I were given the time and good health to fulfill our hope to write this book on self-care. Students at Perkins School of Theology, SMU, have never lost the vision for the need for this book.

In closing, I praise my two adult children, David and Jean Moessner, and my husband, Dave Moessner, for believing that I could ride that pachyderm in Platteville, Wisconsin! They have believed in me, even as I faced elephants!

I write these Acknowledgments on Easter Sunday, 2013. I remain convinced that no matter how huge the challenge, nothing will trample the church triumphant. I am grateful for God's journey mercies.—J.S.M.

As I have worked on this manuscript with Jeanne, I have been reminded continually of the intertwining relationships of body, mind, and spirit, and the centrality of incarnation to our religious, spiritual, professional, and personal lives. Clergy and other religious professionals navigate these relationships daily—a calling and vocation that can be both fulfilling and exhausting. I thank the many pastors and seminarians who have shared their stories and journeys with me over the years for their honesty, vulnerability, and all they have taught me along the way.

I especially appreciate colleagues and friends who have mentored me in my ministry of clergy care and wellness. These include the Rev. Dr. R. Mark Biddle, Dr. Fred Smoot, Dr. Teresa Snorton, the Rev. Pierce W. Klemmt, the Rev. Dr. Joyce Mercer, and the Rev. Dr. Carol Pinkham Oak. I also learned much about systems and denominational issues pertaining to clergy and missionaries during my years of service with Emory Clergy Care, the United Methodist Board of Global Ministries Mission Personnel Resources Program, the Commission on Ministry of the Christian Church (Disciples of Christ), and the clergy residency program at Christ Church, Alexandria, Virginia. Thanks to all!

Like Jeanne, I am grateful to Kathy Armistead at Abingdon—not only for her vision for this book, but also for her patience and understanding during my family's move and at least one computer crash as I was working on this manuscript. Thanks to Jennifer Manley Rogers and her guidance through production, and also to Terri-Lynne Smiles for her wise review and comments about this project.

Jeanne and I have talked about collaborating on a book for at least fifteen years—I cannot thank her enough for inviting me to share in this project, and for her pastoral insights, generosity, and friendship over the years.

And to my husband, David Vandermeulen, and children, Laura and John—the "elephant book" got finished in time for Easter! Thanks for your patience and not begrudging me a few extra hours of computer time!

As I write this on Easter Sunday 2013, I give thanks for all clergy who serve God in the many settings of ministry. Grace, peace, and good health to all! —M.L.D.

PREFACE

A church, synagogue, cathedral, temple, mosque, or parish can be a dangerous place. The hazards often lurk within the religious institution itself. In fact, these perils may be so obvious that they are like "elephants" standing in the fellowship hall, sanctuary, pastor's study, or any room in the church. The word *elephant* stands for an obvious truth or issue that is ignored or unnamed, yet is allowed to occupy a large amount of space in the minds and hearts of those who tiptoe around it. The "elephant" squats in the fellowship hall, but we put the punch and cookies in the corner and carry on light conversation as usual. The "elephant" lumbers around the sanctuary as we worship, yet we try to ignore it and concentrate on the sermon—which, of course, does not mention the "elephant." It is hard to stay focused in the pastor's study, because the "elephant" distracts us from what we really want to say. We keep denying there is a problem with the "elephant" occupying the church because it would upset the way we have all learned to cope and squeeze around it. We guard the children and elderly from being stepped on by the "elephant," all the while remembering how we have been hurt by its presence.

This book may save your life. It could easily save your ministry. There are many reasons for the blinders worn to avoid seeing the "elephants" or the care taken to maneuver around them. Because of this denial and avoidance, we may even come to differing perspectives on the "elephant" in the church. Let us illustrate with a story of blind men and an elephant. This parable originated in India and eventually surfaced in Jain, Buddhist, Sufi, and Hindu traditions. The Jain version described six blind men examining different parts of the elephant's body. The one who touches the leg exclaims that the elephant is like a pillar; the one who feels the tail says the elephant is like a rope; the one feeling the trunk likens the elephant to a tree branch; the one touching the ear compares the elephant to a hand fan; the one feeling the belly pronounces the elephant to be like a wall; the one rubbing the tusk proclaims the elephant to be like a pipe. Their "blindness" prevents the six men from acknowledging the truth before them. In 2010, the pharmaceutical firm Bayer produced an ad showing blindfolded women examining a rhinoceros and drawing different conclusions about the animal. In both the ancient Indian version and the more recent rendition, "the whole picture" eluded the examiners. This book is an exercise in removing the blindfolds that may hinder the health and safety of the church.

Dr. Mary Lynn Dell, psychiatrist and theologian, and Dr. Jeanne Stevenson-Moessner, minister and professor of pastoral care, combine their years of training, areas of expertise, and acquired wisdom to navigate some of the blind spots in ministry. As ministers themselves, Drs. Mary Lynn Dell and Jeanne Stevenson-Moessner have faced "elephants in the church" and advocated for the endangered species: ministers and clergy. Read with caution as you keep one eye on the elephant in the room!

C h a p t e r   O n e

ELEPHANTS

When asked to write this book, I remembered my first personal encounter with a live elephant. I was in second grade and asked to sit atop a husky elephant at the Memphis Zoo. While exciting and scary for me, this was also a photo opportunity for members of the Republican Party. A Memphis newspaper, *The Commercial Appeal*, ran a picture of my hanging on to the pachyderm with grave intensity. The elephant did not feel like what I had imagined. Its skin was oily, almost tender, and its hide was prickly, like the stubble of a beard. I was fascinated with the sheer size and height of this commanding creature. How could anyone overlook seeing that elephant!

Yet, in twenty-five years of teaching in theological institutions, I know it is common to overlook an elephant in the room. By this I do not mean an animal like the one I rode in second grade. I mean an IMMENSE issue or COLOSSAL conflict that is avoided, ignored, or overlooked. I mean a concern that is huge or elephantine. An "elephant in the room" is "metaphorically evocative of any object or matter of which everyone

1

is definitely aware and yet no one is willing to publicly acknowledge."[1] It is to ignore, conceal, deny, hide, or avoid the obvious.

The topic of "elephants" or unnamed issues in the church did not initially evoke within me a positive response. However, when I considered the amount of damage an unrestrained elephant could unleash in a church, I had to reconsider. If provoked or unattended, an elephant can crush things of value and soil our gathering places. Our finely trained seminarians can be endangered in their ministries by collusions and conspiracies to deny or to conceal elephants in the churches. It is for reasons of their safety that I agreed to co-write this book. Interestingly, when I mentioned this writing project to a roomful of theological students at Perkins School of Theology, each student came forth with numerous examples of hidden dangers in ministry. Most of these students are already serving in churches. They have experienced firsthand the dysfunctional ecclesiastical spaces where blindfolds are worn and where blind spots are standard. These students know that a healthy pastor is an endangered species. The drop-out rate and the burn-out rate among ministers has been of concern to all denominations. It is of vital concern to me. Ministers are at great risk for compassion fatigue, an overextension of themselves in their life of service and in their acts of mercy. Often, ministers are expected to do too much and are like lifeguards at a community pool: "Lifeguards take regular breaks, change their viewing stations repeatedly during shifts, and take many other steps to maintain their vigilance, but vigilance, besides being subject to its own limitations, cannot eliminate *inattentional blindness* [emphasis mine]. The lifeguards simply cannot see everything, but the illusion of attention makes us believe they will."[2] A minister cannot see or foresee everything. Inattention to elephants in the room often results in a trampling of the minister underfoot—by accident or by design. Although bush and forest elephants are considered endangered species,[3] that is not the focus of this book. Rather, the focus is on those serving Christ and the church and their imperiled longevity.

The Rat and the Elephant (Adapted from Aesop's Fables)

There was once a rat who sauntered down the road. Suddenly, his vision was blocked by the sight of a lumbering elephant and his entourage. This coterie of admirers included the "royal family" and attendants, a favorite cat and dog, a parrot, and a monkey. Behind these came a group of followers. They blocked the rat's progress. "What fools you are to be devoted to an elephant," the rat blubbered. "Is it his size or bulk that impresses you? That weight will frighten some little boys and girls! I can frighten people, too. I have two eyes, two ears, and four legs like that elephant whom you adore! That elephant has no right to monopolize the highway!" The rat's loud protest drew the attention of the cat. She eyed the rat for a moment, then jumped to the ground, and swiftly showed the rat that he was no elephant.

Many of us have entered an institution where the "presence" of a revered predecessor looms heavily in the halls, the office, the sanctuary, the fellowship hall. The legacy is larger than life and is comparable to the elephant and his entourage in this fable. The predecessor is like a "heavyweight" in the ring of service: the sermons were the most substantial; the bedside manner was life changing; the theology was solid; the building renovations are massive. The successes are frequently recounted with pride. In some denominations, previous pastors are allowed to visit the former congregation/parish. In others, revisiting is discouraged if not prohibited. In this latter case, nevertheless, the "living legend" can still impose his or her presence on the incoming pastor or priest or rabbi.

Rachel knew she was in trouble. She was fifty-two, in a second career, well trained in a prominent theological institution, and totally unprepared for the "apparition" in her first full-time appointment. Now, Rachel had been an outstanding student, earning a preaching award at graduation. Her first career was in communications; she was an able speaker. She was biblically grounded, theologically astute, and trained in conflict resolution. She was an A student in all her pastoral care courses. However, theological education did not prepare her for the imposing presence of her predecessor, Rev. Wayne Bright, now in early retirement in an assisted living facility near Crossroads United Methodist (UMC), a small-town church. Rev. Bright had suffered a massive heart attack and currently resided with his devoted wife in Shady Grove Retirement Village. Some longtime parishioners, speaking with a reverent lilt in their voices, were convinced that dear Rev. Bright had so loved their church, that it almost killed him!

Unless it was a new member or a new family, Rev. Bright was always requested for weddings, funerals, and baptisms of grandchildren. Rachel assisted, of course, but the longtime congregants wanted dear Rev. Bright. He and Mrs. Bright attended church almost every Sunday, and the congregation clustered around them at the coffee hour. It also followed that before surgeries and after accidents, the established members wanted the prayers of Rev. Bright. Rachel felt that the road to her ministry was blocked by Rev. Bright's imposing entourage and admirers. He was like the elephant in Aesop's fable. Rachel knew that to challenge this dotage on Rev. Bright would result in a counterattack, as the cat pounced on the rat.

She was not Rev. Bright. She knew her greatest gift was in preaching. The content and application of her sermons were well received. Even so, she overheard criticisms of her delivery: she left the pulpit and "wandered" around the chancel. Rachel used a narrative style that was unfamiliar, given Rev. Bright's three-point, deductive sermons. If her strength in preaching was not appreciated, what chance did she have to succeed with the elephantine specter of Rev. Bright that lumbered around the church?

Rachel began to research the history of this local UMC church. Fortunately, as in most churches, there was a resident historian. There were church records in the library, but the oral history proved equally significant. The church had suffered a great tragedy in Rev. Bright's time of leadership; Bright had been reappointed to this congregation by the bishop after the accident. The youth of the church were on a mission trip to Mexico and were staying with a UMC congregation near the U.S./Mexican border. The young people were staying in the church gym when one teenager swung from the basketball goal. The heavy upright goal toppled and fell onto the chest of the teenager. He died later that night in the hospital. This incident became a permanent scar in the life of this church. The youth group disbanded. The entire congregation was enveloped in a profound grief. Rev. Bright saw them through the rawest stages of pain. He suffered alongside as a good pastor would. He was part of their recovery and of a past they shared.

Rachel decided to enter this past. She essentially reposi-
tioned herself to be "at the head of the procession." The new
family center was soon to be five years old. Rachel initiated
a potluck supper in honor of the building's anniversary with
Rev. and Mrs. Bright as special guests. The resident historian of Crossroads UMC was invited to give a history of the
building of the center. This included mention of the tragic
accident, which resulted in the memorial gifting of funds
and programs for this new building. Working with the elders
and the Brights, Rachel proposed a summer camp for local
youth and enlisted the aid of the leaders in her parish. The
camp would be named in memory of their "lost son." In this
way, Rachel stepped into the prolonged parade of grief in
that church and pointed in a new direction. If we refer to
Aesop's fable, the rat now leads the caravan of elephant, attendants, and admirers in a new and healthier direction. As
a postscript, when Rachel was eventually appointed by the
bishop to another church, Crossroads UMC lamented the loss
of Rachel so greatly that they have elevated her to the position
of a saint!

The Lion, Jupiter, and the Elephant
(Adapted from Aesop's Fables)

Elephants from the past come in so many guises. In Rachel's story, it was a revered predecessor. The congregation
used two psychological processes to elevate this minister: idealization and idolization. Idealization is the exclusive selection
of positive attributes and affirming memories; these attributes
and memories are the only lens through which a person or
situation is viewed. Idolization is the exaltation of a person,
issue, or party to the point of worship.

Elephants from the pastor's past can also roam the rooms of the church. For example, a brutal divorce, an extramarital affair, or a suspicion of inappropriate sexual activity can result in silence and denial. In his book *The Elephant in the Room: Silence and Denial in Everyday Life*,[4] sociologist Eviatar Zerubavel describes the role of the closemouthed bystanders, who by their very silence enable the denial. Meta-denial is the denial of the denial.[5] This can happen to the individual, to the congregation, or to a group within the congregation. Silence then becomes a source of fear.[6] When an elephant is surrounded by expressed or suppressed fear, even the tiniest gnat can undo it.

In Aesop's *The Lion, Jupiter, and the Elephant*, the lion is complaining to the god Jupiter that he, the stout lion, is frightened by the crowing of a cock. Although the lion is handsome, strong, and powerful, he is bothered by this one fear. Jupiter is not sympathetic and recounts all the marvelous attributes that he had given the lion. Shortly thereafter, the lion encounters an elephant. The elephant is constantly shaking his head and ears. His ears move with a tremor. Just at that moment, the lion spots a gnat on the head of the elephant. The elephant confesses: "Do you see that tiny gnat? If it enters my ear, my fate is sealed, and I shall die!" The lion reflects on this predicament and concludes, "If such a huge beast is terrified of a gnat, I'll stop complaining. I am better off than the elephant!"

Flute

Denial of an elephant in the church and silence surrounding it can create a precarious situation. Pastor Richard Leifker was appointed to a church that had a history of unhealthy interpersonal boundaries. The church had never dealt with previous innuendos of impropriety and inappropriate behavior. Pastor Leifker was still in theological training when he asked for help with the following situation:

A three-year-old girl named Tammy goes to preschool in a Methodist church. Tammy is an only child. Preschool is Wednesdays and Fridays from 8:30 a.m. to 2 p.m. At 9:30 on Wednesdays, the children go to a 30-minute chapel time. They wear a blue uniform shirt on their chapel days. Pastor Richard is not leading the children in chapel on this particular chapel day. He arrives at church just after the service.

After chapel on this particular day, the children go into the large room across from the pastor's office, where "Ernie the music man" has brought in musical instruments of every kind for the children to play. Tammy secures the flute to play because she has one at home and knows how to "play" it. Evidently, she goes over near the pastor's door to play so he will hear it. The church is filled with the "music" of drums, horns, guitars, etc.

On Friday, Tammy's mother decides to have Tammy wear the blue uniform shirt to preschool. The child objects to the shirt. She says she does not want to go to chapel. (Note: the shirt and chapel are associated with one another.) Mother gets another shirt.

Between Friday and Monday, Tammy and her mother talk. Tammy's mother hears her say, "Pastor hurt me with the red flute." Tammy's mother does not question any further, but she goes to the school on Tuesday. (Note: school is closed on Monday.) She talks to the director of the preschool. Again, the mother says she believes the child told her, "The pastor hurt me with the red flute." Pastor Richard is notified. A meeting is called.

At this point, Pastor Richard confided in me this chain of events. As open communication took place and as events were reconstructed, it was clear that Tammy had said, "The pastor heard me with the red flute." Pastor Richard continued to maintain clear and firm boundaries as he had always done. In this case and in all churches, knowledge of the past history of the congregation is vital, lest a "gnat" of gossip or misunderstanding seal the fate of the church or the minister.

All Creatures, Great and Small

An elephant is one of the greater, or larger, creatures that God has made. An elephant is not an evil animal. In fact, many of us were raised on children's stories featuring kind and talented elephants. One popular narrative features Dumbo, who is ridiculed from birth because he has such large and floppy ears. In the circus, his mother tries to protect him from bullying and teasing, but she is soon separated from him. One friend, Timothy, remains faithful to little Dumbo. They accidentally drink champagne one evening, become inebriated, and wake up in a tree. It is discovered that Dumbo has flown them there! When Dumbo's aerial arts are discovered by the circus owners, he becomes the star attraction. Kind Dumbo forgives all his former tormentors and is reunited with his mother. What child cannot identify with the need for protection and acceptance?

In 1931, Jean de Brunhoff introduced a winsome and orphaned baby elephant named Babar in *The Story of Babar*. After Babar ran away from the hunter who killed his mother, he came upon a town. Babar showed courage in maneuvering his way through town and skill in adapting to clothes, friendships, and language. Eventually, Babar left the city to return to the forest, where he was elected king of the elephants. Subsequent adventures of Babar were written by de Brunhoff and his son, Laurent, but were always illustrated with Babar in a bright green suit and a bowler hat, accoutrements that brought a smile to young readers.

Elephants come in many shapes and sizes, but whether weighing seven tons (African elephant) or six tons (Asian elephant), they are the largest of the living land mammals. They are feared and revered. They have been used in warfare; Hannibal used them to defeat the Romans in 219 BC on the banks of the Trebia River. They have been used in entertainment, particularly as circus performers and beasts of burden. In 1882, P. T. Barnum bought an elephant named Jumbo from the London Zoo; Jumbo was a famous attraction until his untimely death. He was mourned worldwide.

An elephant is a complicated creature. Sara Gruen's *Water for Elephants*[7] develops this intricate makeup in the character of Rosie, an elephant in the Benzini Brothers Circus. Rosie is intelligent, resilient, and capable of devotion. She suffers from a violent owner/trainer. When the violence is turned on her rider, Rosie kills the owner in defense.

Elephants in the church are not physical or fictional animals but rather larger-than-life issues that loom in our midst. They can be as varied and as complex as the fictional (Dumbo) and actual (Jumbo). Elephants can be innocuous; they can be entertaining; they can be deadly. In the church, they can be used in warfare. The purpose of this book is to demonstrate how to identify elephants in the church and to lead them out of the sacred space. To do this, you will become an "elephant rider," one who can sensitively and appropriately maneuver the elephantine issues that threaten to trample the life of the church.

Elephant Rider

My daughter reminded me of the second time I rode an elephant. This second time did not provoke fear in me, and I had temporarily forgotten it. It was in 1997, in Platteville, Wisconsin, when Disney on Parade came to the small town. Each year, one small town was chosen as the site for the extravaganza. Our two children were in kindergarten and third grade, so my husband and I took them to Platteville. There was a parade down the main street with lots of Disney characters, floats, and music. What my daughter seems to remember best is the ride on the elephant after the parade.

The elephant rides were in a park near the center of town. We waited in line, paid for tickets, and mounted some wooden steps to a platform built on top of the massive elephant. The platform astride the elephant was secured by ropes under his belly and roped off so children would be safe. I asked my daughter if she was frightened. She said the animal was BIG, but she knew she wouldn't fall off. Unlike my own experience as a child, where I literally and figuratively had no grasp of the situation, in Platteville, we were elephant riders on a predictable route with appropriate boundaries and controls.

This is what we are about with this book. We cannot eliminate the unavoidable issues and obstacles in the church. But we can pay attention to them, name them, guide them, secure them, and eventually control the direction of their gait.

Here is one example of a graduate from a Protestant seminary becoming an "elephant rider."[8] Paula took four years to complete seminary. She was mentored in her third year by a visiting professor of Christian education. This professor literally and metaphorically rearranged the furniture in the classroom through experiential and participatory learning. This was in the late 1980s, when most classroom seating arrangements were in straight rows, set up for lectures and deductive learning. This visiting professor redid the seating arrangement and made circular patterns in which students could really see each other. Paula learned a methodology that included truth telling without breaching confidentiality, creation of a safe space, assertiveness, reliance on internal authority, listening, non-dichotomizing the sacred and the profane, networking, and empowerment of the constituency.

Paula's task following seminary was to translate this methodology into her ministry. Paula chose a troubled, dysfunctional church. She was and is in a denomination in which a minister and the congregation choose each other. I don't know why Paula chose a dying and abused congregation. A former minister, who was later imprisoned for eighteen months for his criminal behavior, had molested children in this church. This history of molestation occurred twelve years prior to Paula's coming to the church, but it was STILL THE ELEPHANT in the midst of any gathering. Where two or three were gathered together, there stood the invisible elephant. It did not help that the minister before the child molester was involved in financial fraud. Perhaps there were TWO ELEPHANTS in the fellowship hall!

After a year in this first pastorate, Paula entered into therapy to take care of herself. She was in a high-risk situation in which even a veteran pastor could be trampled to death. I interviewed Paula three and a half years into her ministry. She considered her ministry successful because she had learned how to train or ride the elephant. First, she seized the power, the reins of the elephant. She took control as an ecclesial authority with the clear vision of restoring the control to her people. She rearranged the furniture and empowered the congregation. She put the pews in a circle and brought the lectern down to their level. She taught them to pay attention to their surroundings; she broke the silence around the elephant of abuse. She reviewed their history with them. She listened to the hushed voices. She listened to the silence before the speaking.[9] From the pulpit, she named the elephants in their history. She modeled truth telling. She became the church's advocate on various issues in presbytery.

I believe Paula's courage was greatest when she planned a healing service for her congregation. Fourteen parishioners volunteered to "carry the pain" of the congregation and stood on behalf of other survivors. These fourteen volunteers told the stories of abuse and recorded them for the first time in the church's minutes. They "rewrote their story" to name the evil. They ritualized it; they redeemed it. Old pairs of shoes were dumped in a pile to represent a worn-out part of the journey, now over. The journey was not over by any means, but the part of their journey that had defined who they were as "abused and downtrodden" was finished. The elephants were not a part of the future journey.

Paula reflected again on the impact of her feminist professor of Christian education. "We knew in the middle of the semester . . . we had been placed in her care . . . an incredible moment when you know something miraculous is happening. She had this way of pottering around and appearing to be doing nothing, yet she was doing so much." She was teaching her students how to ride an elephant.

Chapter Two

A HERD OF ELEPHANTS

*"I have seen a herd of Elephant traveling through dense native forest . . .
pacing along as if they had an appointment at the end of the world."*
—*Isak Dinesen,* Out of Africa

It would seem difficult to miss a herd of elephants. We discussed in chapter 1 the matter of inattentive "blindness." Perhaps you are in the forest and tending to a bruised knee, or a small child, and your attention is diverted. Perhaps you are in a patch of sunlight, temporarily "blinded" by the illumination of the sun, and visually unable to discern the herd of elephants moving rapidly through the shadowy foliage.

As I was writing this chapter, this tragedy was announced in my local newspaper: "86-year-old Pedestrian Struck and Killed by Van."[1] A woman was hit on the main street of a small village named Blanchardville, Wisconsin, while she was crossing at 8:15 in the morning. Another resident of this small community, a thirty-two-year-old man, was travelling south on Main Street and "was unable to avoid hitting her." He was cited by the Lafayette County Sheriff's Department with "inattentive driving." The accident is being investigated. In addition to the possibilities of preoccupation and distraction, let us consider for a moment temporary blindness: "Our visual system's sensitivity is at the mercy of variable environmental conditions."[2] Our visual system must be capable of adjusting to the daily cycle of illumination in the day and darkness at night. Notice that the accident occurred at 8:15 a.m. The van was travelling south. Was the woman crossing from east to west? Did the sunlight on this July morning blind the driver? "[W]hen the change of overall illumination is sudden or very rapid, our visual system's adaptive mechanisms respond too sluggishly to keep up with the change, thus rendering us temporarily 'blind' until the adjustment problem has been completed."[3] Was the pedestrian outside the driver's peripheral vision when he perhaps curved slightly at a bend in the road? Or was the driver preoccupied with a cup of cappuccino? These are all questions I would ask if part of the investigative team.

Ministers seek to steer or guide their churches. It is vital that we as religious professionals be aware of our blind spots, our limited vision, our distractions and preoccupations. Inattention to any of these can be fatal to us and our ministry. The following case is a tragic account of the death of Rev. Philip Strong, who did not foresee impending disaster.

The Crucifixion of Philip Strong

Rev. Philip Strong was a gifted orator at the turn of the twentieth century. He turned down an invitation to take a university church, Chapel Hill Church in Elmdale, although he "had an inclination . . . toward a quiet, scholarly pastorate."[4] Instead, Philip Strong chose Calvary Church in Milton: "a noisy, dirty, manufacturing town" filled with mill workers, sixty saloons, six churches on the main street, and a powerful ruling class.[5] As you may have guessed, most of the "leading families" were members of his new church; this included the major property owners of the mills, tenements, and saloons. Unlike his well-liked predecessor, Dr. Brown, who did not "mix" religion and social ethics, Rev. Philip Strong decided to preach a series on "Christ and Modern Society."[6] He did so on the first Sunday of each month. Unlike his predecessor, he would name the elephants in his own church: greed, corruption, unethical business practices, gambling, exploitation of the working class, and prostitution.

On the first Sunday in the series, Strong preached on the "Right and Wrong Uses of Property." His congregation sat stunned, because most of the wealthy property owners were sitting in front of him. The next day, an irate Mr. William Winter came calling at the manse; Mr. Winter was chairman of the board of trustees of the church and had walked out of the church in the middle of the sermon. Mr. Winter owned most of the buildings that were rented out by saloon keepers. Mr. Winter threatened the preacher and admonished him, telling him not to pry into people's business. Mr. Winter stated that he would withdraw his support, presence, *and* money from Calvary Church if Rev. Strong continued with this meddling.

The burden of fighting these elephants by himself began to wear on Rev. Strong. Yet he continued in his series, tackling "the demon rum" and the saloons that corrupted the working-class families, especially in the tenements. Although Calvary Church was packed due to the sensationalism of the sermon series, the tension among the membership was palpable. Shortly thereafter, while leaving the manse at night to make a visit to a sick child, Rev. Strong was shot twice, in the knee and in the shoulder. He got a glimpse of the face of the shooter in the lamplight. It was one of the saloon owners.

While convalescing for three weeks, Rev. Strong read all the newspapers and newsletters of the mill town. He noticed that not only shops but gambling houses, saloons, and places of prostitution were open on Sundays. This desacralized the Sabbath, although his church was increasing in attendance. Mind you, he did not have the majority sympathy of his congregation; it was the force and passionate delivery of his sermons that drew the crowds. There were a few people who supported him, but Rev. Strong essentially faced the elephants alone: undue power of Christian landowners, the financial strangulation of the poor, subhuman living conditions in the tenements, the unregulated grip of "the demon rum," and the separation of personal ethics and one's faith.

Rev. Strong's home was vandalized; a knife and threatening letters were left on his desk. Still, he persisted in his ministry. He had named vices, and now members who supported these vices were angry. They organized like a herd and were ready to stampede. The strain of the impending onslaught even took its toll on his body. But there were also individuals whom he deeply affected in a positive way by his ministry, including, eventually, Mr. Winter, chairman of the board of trustees. Other "leading" members of the congregation, however, charged like trampling elephants, as if they had a date with the end of the world.

On that last Sunday, in the middle of his delivery, Strong staggered back from the lectern, threw his arms up, and extended one long arm toward a Latin cross on the rear wall of the church: "For one intense tremendous second of time he stood there with the whole church smitten into a pitying, horrified, startled, motionless crowd of blanched staring faces, as his tall, dark figure towered up with outstretched arms, almost covering the very outlines of the cross, and then he sank at its foot."[7]

His funeral was held in Milton, where "rugged, unfeeling men were seen to cry like children in the streets. A great procession, largely made up of the poor and sinful, followed him to his wintry grave."[8] His wife exclaimed, "They [the unsympathetic parishioners] killed him!"[9]

A Modern Rendition: The Survival of Deaconess Dorothy

While the story of Rev. Philip Strong occurred in 1899, the same dynamics still occur today. A theology student I shall call Dorothy told me a similar story. She was a deaconess whose church in 2010 survived an ordeal reminiscent of the travail of Calvary Church.

Her church was in an affluent section of a major city in Texas. In the early 1970s, the membership hovered around eighteen hundred. Two universities were nearby. Most parishioners were affluent African-Americans, as was Dorothy. With the influx of other ethnicities, particularly Hispanic, the neighborhood began to change. Many among the established membership left the church when they moved out of the neighborhood. At the time Dorothy told me the history of her church, the membership was down to two hundred members on the roll. On any given Sunday, eighty-eight were in worship. The average age was sixty-two.

Dorothy had been in ministry for seven years, five of those in children's ministry. She, the pastors, and the members of her church perceived the call of God for them to stay in their location. Their focus was similar to Rev. Strong's: "Christ in modern society."

But there was a threat looming from outside the congregation. The Methodist Conference decided to close the church for fear that apportionments or connectional budgets would not be met, because Methodist churches must contribute to governance structures in regional districts called conferences. The conference had particular ideas about the "right and wrong uses of property," and Dorothy's church could affect the flow of money if unable to pay their apportionment. This would impact the conference's ability to meet financial obligations. While Dorothy's church was doing vital ministry, wealthier congregations were the leaders of the denomination and often controlled the conference's decision-making process.

Rev. Strong fought the elephants in his church and was trampled to death. How could Dorothy's church survive? They fought the denominational pressures and finally prevailed, keeping their church open. Both Rev. Strong and Dorothy had vision. Both had determination and passion. Both believed that they were doing God's ministry. Both had formidable obstacles against a stampede of resistance. Dorothy wanted to tell her story because it was one of anxiety, fear, and finally survival. How did she triumph?

From the very beginning of her narrative, it was clear that Dorothy did not stand alone. She, along with the other pastors and the congregation, made a united resistance. After all, a "herd of elephants" was outside the church doors. Destruction of this neighborhood church was imminent. But when the fears were named, these fears were faced not in isolation, but in community.

Naming the ecclesiastical representatives as the elephants in this analogy is not to pass judgment on them or make them into demons. They were only doing their job as they saw it. After all, an elephant is part of God's creation; it is even revered in some cultures. But a herd of elephant can be dangerous if its path crosses yours, especially if it has "an appointment with the end of the world."

A Herd of Elephants: Family Systems Perspective

One approach to understanding the way we act and function in our places of ministry is called family systems theory. This theory offers a lens through which we can view our role as one member of a complex system called the "family." The family can be much like a herd, where there is lack of self-differentiation between the individual member of the herd and the herd itself. The religious professional operates in the vortex of three "family systems," or herds: 1) his or her own family of origin, that is, the family into which he or she was adopted, born, or fostered; 2) the church or religious organization as a family of faith or affiliation; 3) the various families that comprise the religious organization, church, synagogue, mosque, and so on. It is very easy to have blind spots within any family, especially when there is overinvolvement, enmeshment, or fusion. All of these terms imply that there is a blurring of personal boundaries; it is hard to tell where "I" as an individual exist distinctly in the "we-ness" of a family or herd.

In the memoir of faith titled *Leaving Church,* author and Episcopal priest Barbara Brown Taylor exposes the blind spots that "the inexplicable alchemy of compassion" allows.[10] She assumed the role of rescuer and describes the burden of this as such: "I had such a strong instinct for rescue that my breasts fairly leaked when I came across those in need of rescuing."[11] Furthermore, she assumed a double role of being married to husband Ed and to the church: "I had been careful to marry him before I married the church, but neither of us had a clue how this blended family was going to work."[12] This blended family overlapped the church family and her married life with Ed. Then, Taylor grew to assume the role of single parent to the church, especially when God seemed absent to her parishioners: "On my worst nights I lay in bed feeling like a single parent . . . for many people God was the parent who had left. . . . Because I was wedded to the One who was gone, I stood in for him."[13]

Family systems theory teaches us to observe our sibling position within our family of origin. In Barbara Brown Taylor's family of origin, she was the eldest of three girls. Ministry attracts firstborn children, only children, or those who function as firstborns. In the latter case, for example, there may be a gap of ten to fifteen years between a group of siblings and a child born later in a marriage or remarriage. The child born much later functions as a firstborn, because the older children have gone or are poised to leave. Firstborns can often assume the role of extraordinary caretaker, rescuer, or savior. I do not know Barbara Brown Taylor's family of origin, but I know mine. I am also the eldest of three, and I easily assume the role of caretaker in ministry. Caretaking and the compassion that accompanies it can certainly be an asset in ministry. Excessive caretaking and over-functioning, however, can led to compassion fatigue, a tiredness that halts one's ministry. A pattern of constantly rescuing others can lead to their underfunctioning. When we play savior, we have usurped the authority of another.

Cases in Point: An Elephant-Sized Job

Both of Mac's parents had been in helping professions. His mother had been a pediatrician, and his father was a social worker in a small town in Texas. Mac was the firstborn of four children. He was taught to be responsible and to watch over his younger siblings. He recalled a vivid memory from when he was eleven. His siblings had rearranged his dad's woodpile to make a fort in the backyard. His father was irate when he saw the disorder. He commanded Mac, "Clean it up." Mac honestly replied, "But I didn't do it. They [his brothers and sister] did it." His dad retorted, "I didn't ask you who did it. I said, 'Clean it up.'" Mac did.

His parents provided every material need for their children. Some of their favorite maxims were as follows: "If it is to be, it is up to me." "What is worth doing is worth doing well." "Cleanliness is next to godliness." "Don't let the sun go down on your wrath." "If you can't say something nice, don't say anything at all." These messages became a heavy load for Mac to carry.

Mac felt called into parish ministry. He was United Methodist (UMC) and was placed in a medium-sized congregation as solo pastor. The church had started a building campaign two years earlier, but with the recession, the goal had not been met. There was dissatisfaction among the members, especially the younger families, who looked forward to a family center in the new building. The church secretary's extramarital affair with a church member had just been revealed. The morale was low among the church leaders. Mac noticed they were always late for their meetings, which he read as passive aggressiveness.

Mac was already feeling overwhelmed when one of his brothers called with bad news. Their younger brother was clearly an alcoholic. Their sister was caught with drugs. Mac now went on high alert. After all, the responsibility for his brothers and sister had always fallen on him. The church family needed him, too. All of the voices of the past asserted themselves, especially "If it is to be, it is up to me."

If anything tramples Mac in ministry, it will be the elephant-sized "job" he has undertaken. Mac was wise enough to seek counseling, where he is learning to *reframe* the voices from his childhood. For "If it is to be, it is up to me," Mac has substituted, "If it is to be, it is up to God. I and others will help." To replace the perfectionist undertones of "What is worth doing is worth doing well," Mac suggests, "What is worth doing is worth doing with the best resources available."

In the elephant-sized job of ministry, a horde of emotions, such as the need to feel needed, can start a stampede. George Hunt relates how this need for affirmation along with an overly zealous work ethic caused him to leave ministry. He is a firstborn child.

> I was excited about my first full-time ministry position in the summer of 1990. I established patterns of work and life that would be my pattern until I left that church six years later. I worked fifty to sixty hours per week, took on enormous responsibility, and sought single-handedly to en-

ergize a church that had been in decline for many years. I was successful, and although I did good work in that place, it came at a significant price as I left the ministry in 1996. After only six years, I had burned out and felt that I had nothing to give.

Although I had been afforded four weeks of vacation per year, I rarely took more than two. I had a day off each week, but usually at least went by the church for two or three hours or more on my days off just to "check on things." When I did get away, I felt a huge sense of relief and was hardly ready to get back. I loved the work, but the work was eating me alive, and I was so young and inexperienced that I didn't realize it. The more I worked, the more I felt my "need to be needed," and the congregation was more than happy to let me overwork. In fact they came to expect it.

When I left the ministry in 1996, I never intended to return. What happened over the course of the next seven years was a sense of healing and call that convinced me that I did in fact belong in ministry, and I needed to handle that call to ministry in a very different way. In 2003, I answered the call to ministry at a church. By this time, I had a growing family. I made it clear to the church from the beginning that I would reserve time for family, but also made a promise to myself to set aside time *for me*. In practice, this covenant has required tremendous discipline, but I find that the rewards of self-care far outweigh the cost of burnout.

An important key to my personal journey in self-care is the understanding of what is important and what is urgent. In Charles Hummel's book *Tyranny of the Urgent!*, the author describes what all of us in ministry feel—that there aren't enough hours in the day.[14] In a church, there are so many things that can fill our days, but the question for Hummel boils down to this: is it important, or is it urgent? When we're constantly living our lives in pursuit of the urgent themes, we often lose track of the important. This had been my pattern in the first chapter of my ministry.

As George put it, he had to work on the puritanical roots of work ethic coupled with a strong dose of "need to be needed." He revised his understanding as a United Methodist of what is meant by the doctrine of sanctification, or the call to be perfect as God is perfect. He concluded, "In our quest to be perfected in love, we must learn to love ourselves perfectly also." How do we love ourselves as God has loved us? "It is a hard fact to swallow that I did not care for myself adequately in my first ministry because I didn't love myself completely, but this is true."

An "elephant-sized job" such as ministry is an arena in which we could be trampled to death. There are hordes of personal issues that can stampede our thoughts and trample our best efforts in ministry. Among this horde are perfectionism, over-functioning, co-dependency, a "savior" or rescue mentality, a low self-image, a need to be needed, an overinflated self-image, and a desire to please. A mention of these tendencies is not an attempt to minimize the risks or to be reductionistic by internalizing the source of the danger of a spiritual stampede. Rather, it is an attempt to acknowledge the complexity of all the factors impinging on a minister's attempt to function well in an elephant-sized job.

The Herd Instinct

The individual stands in a complex network of systems: an ecological system, a political system, an organizational system, an environmental system. In addition, within every person's body, there are systems: circulatory, respiratory, neurological, vascular, skeletal. In a psychological approach to understanding the individual in a vortex of relationships, we study the "family system." We begin with the family of origin, the family from which the individual came or was raised. The family of origin can be constructed through biology, adoption (informal and formal), fosterage, and step-parenting. One of the most intriguing questions that can be asked in the study of one's genealogy, or family tree, is the question "Who ordained you?"

At first, when this question is asked, there is often a reaction of offense. Why, of course God ordained us! That statement is surely correct. If a seminarian or ordained person looks back at his or her family tree, however, there is "someone who ordained them." This research may require going back at least three generations, that is, to great-grandparents. But that person will be discovered, along with the realization that he or she blessed you and prepared the way for your call to ministry. Try it!

One of the most famous examples is that of Dr. Martin Luther King, Jr. According to King, he was religious. He grew up in the church. His father was a preacher, his grandfather was a preacher, his great-grandfather was a preacher, his only brother was a preacher, his daddy's brother was a preacher. So, according to how he thought about it, he didn't have much choice.[15] Thus, King's family tree yielded these preachers: Rev. (Michael) Martin Luther King, Sr. (father), who pastored Ebenezer Baptist Church; Rev. Adam David Williams (maternal grandfather), who founded Ebenezer Baptist Church; Willis Williams (maternal great-grandfather), Baptist minister; Alfred Daniel (AD) King (brother), who pastored Ebenezer

Baptist Church; and a paternal uncle who was a preacher. Alberta Williams, Martin Luther King's mother, was the choir director at Ebenezer Baptist; she was shot in 1974 while at her organ.

Martin Luther King was a middle child and excelled at bringing others together: "middle children become outstanding collaborative leaders because they can draw together multiple factions through collaboration and mediation."[16] Martin Luther King's passion for nonviolent group resistance and his tactic of "joining forces" are a "good fit with this sibling position."[17] While some people feel fated by circumstances to take their path in life, others feel called, or "ordained," by their family of origin. The latter is true of Dr. Martin Luther King.

The "herd instinct" is to stay true to the "herd," or family. Some individuals attempt this at great personal cost. In Flannery O'Connor's novel *Wise Blood*, Hazel Motes desperately wants to be a circuit preacher like his grandfather, who is described as "a waspish old man who had ridden over three counties with Jesus hidden in his head like a stinger."[18] Haze (Hazel) was a firstborn child who had had two brothers. One died in infancy, the other in a mowing machine accident. Haze was haunted with dreams of being in a coffin; he recalled vividly his grandfather's preaching of sin and damnation. On Saturdays in Eastrod, Tennessee, his preacher grandfather used him as an example of depravity: "The old man would point to his grandson, Haze. He had a particular disrespect for him because his own face was repeated almost exactly in the child's and seemed to mock him."[19] Did the crowd know that Jesus would die for even a sinful, dirty, unthinking boy like that? Even ten million deaths for such a lost soul?[20] Haze didn't need to hear these words of damnation:

There was already a deep black wordless conviction in him that the way to avoid Jesus was to avoid sin. He knew by the time he was twelve years old that he was going to be a preacher. Later he saw Jesus move from tree to tree in the back of his mind, a wild ragged figure motioning him to turn around and come off into the dark where he was not sure of his footing, where he might be walking on the water and not know it and then suddenly know it and drown.[21]

Haze begins to dodge Jesus. His torturous mission in life is to found "The Church Without Christ," an ecclesiastical structure without the ragged redeemer who haunted his mind. Haze Motes dies in poverty, loneliness, and blindness. He died looking for a "new Jesus" upon which to found his new church. Who ordained Haze to this mission?

From a family systems perspective, it is imperative that we look at the messages passed down from generation to generation in our families of origin. These messages can shape us for better or worse. As we acknowledge the influence of "the herd," or family of origin, upon us, we can better engage in a journey of self-differentiation. To me, self-differentiation is becoming all that God created me to be. It requires an honest appraisal of the damaging messages that drift like a bad odor through family gatherings. It includes claiming models of strength and courage. Self-differentiation can be likened to the spiritual process of sanctification, in which we grow in God's love and into our healthy potential. It is the opposite of the stunted and mangled attempts of Haze Motes to escape damnation. Rather, self-differentiation is a movement toward amazing grace.

White Elephants

In one of the seminaries where I taught, there was a Christmas party each year with a "white elephant exchange." This was a time to get rid of some ugly, unwanted, hideous object. We called them "white elephants." You just hoped someone in the room had not given that item to you as a genuine gift on another occasion! The objects were always covered, so you never knew what was inside a beautifully wrapped package. One year I got a volume on *Pathological Sex Play*! That was embarrassing. Another year, I got a set of china coffee mugs with the face of the seminary dean on each one. It appears his church in Seattle had ordered these as mementos of his time as pastor. I had the remainder of the supply, which the dean actually wanted. I ended up giving him my "white elephant."

Coming into a new church is a lot like drawing a white elephant gift, which comes in an attractive package that does not reveal its contents in the selection stage. White elephants that are passed on to us in ministry include packages of racism, power struggles, abuse, financial situations (especially deficits and building projects), and feuding families. Family systems, as a theory or approach to social processes, teaches us that we are parts of three families: our family of origin, the church as a family, and the individual families within the "church family." As ministers, we are working out of the interface of all three, and this intersection can be a tricky convergence to navigate. For example, in his book on antagonists in the church, Kenneth Haugk warns us about the white elephant called "the instant buddy flag":

> Be cautious with those who relate to you in an overly
> friendly fashion as soon as you move to a new congregation

or immediately after they transfer into your congregation. When you first arrive, these individuals might be among the first to invite you to dinner. While you are together, antagonists will characteristically spend much time and effort probing you and trying to become intimately acquainted. Later, their inquisitiveness will turn to the proverbially cool contempt bred of familiarity.[22]

How do we discern whether a gesture or invitation is a white elephant, as Haugk portends, or a genuine show of the biblical gift of hospitality?

Wisdom is a by-product of this process of pastoral maturity, the development of self-differentiation. The maintenance of healthy boundaries between self and others allows one to recognize a white elephant for what it is. The book on sexual pathology is still on my office bookshelf, and I laugh when I see it. The china cups with the dean's face on them were given to their rightful owner. Maintaining clear boundaries in the game of white elephants allows the pastor to be a non-anxious presence, even a playful presence at times.

In the Hindu pantheon of gods, Ganesha is depicted with an elephant head or heads. Ganesha, the remover of obstacles and a source of beginnings, has also been depicted with five elephant heads. The gift of a white elephant as we have used the term in this chapter can be an obstacle to be removed. It can also herald a new beginning, because the recipient has the power to give it away. In chapter 3, we shall unwrap some white elephants.

Stampede (or, "You Have Destroyed Our Sweet Little Church")

"Elephants will leave you alone if you don't bother them," a sheik once told me on the banks of the Blue Nile. "They left my father alone, and his father before him."
—Alfred Edmund Brehm"

They had left the former pastor alone, and the pastor before him. Of course, these two previous pastors had never dealt with troubling issues. Then Reverend Sheila was appointed by the United Methodist Church (UMC) to this urban church in a large city in Pennsylvania. Reverend Sheila described herself as sixty-one, white-haired, and destined for a rural appointment. But then she spoke with her district superintendent (DS) and asked for a church in the city. She was excited by this church (Moody Methodist) because she "sensed a hunger for the Word of God." The members were very receptive to her preaching. Reverend Sheila chose "theme preaching" and worked through all twelve of the steps used by Alcoholics Anonymous. She used the steps as a "guide for how the church ought to look." That is when the stampede began.

At this point in the book, try to find the elephants in the following build-up to the stampede. Perhaps you have seen the children's book *Where's Waldo?*[1] In that elaborately illustrated book, the young man Waldo is camouflaged by a vast array of people and items on any given page. The challenge is to locate Waldo, who is cleverly hidden. In similar fashion, can you locate the elephants in the disarray in Reverend Sheila's church?

"Our Sweet Little Church"

When Reverend Sheila arrived at the church, attendance was around forty to fifty each Sunday. There was a part-time organist and a part-time director of music, Fred. Fred had been employed for twenty years there and worked six hours a week for an annual salary of $21,000. Fred would often ask soloists to sing when he was out of town, and at those times the choir was not needed. He had dropped bell choir and the youth music ministry, and he now concentrated solely on the adult choir. Besides Fred, there are some others you will need to know in this "sweet little church":

- Corinne, head of administrative council for more than ten years, matriarch of the church

- Mike, treasurer, member of finance committee, head of trustees for more than forty years, patriarch of the church

- Martha, member of finance committee, new member of church

- Dale, chair of staff parish relations committee

- Cheryl, administrative assistant

When Reverend Sheila was considering this appointment, the current minister of Moody Methodist was being transferred to a large church. He said to Sheila, "[Moody] is a great appointment. This is the easiest place to serve you will ever have." He played golf a lot and went to sports events. He put in minimal hours at the church and let the administrative assistant leave early. He mentioned to Sheila that she would really enjoy working with Mike: "This older man [age eighty-nine] is so much fun."

Sheila had such hopes for the church. When the administrative assistant would try to leave early, Sheila asked her to keep regular hours. The administrative assistant quit. Sheila hired a competent woman with two seminary degrees who was not yet ordained; this woman became a steadying influence in the church office and "had Sheila's back."

Sheila made a few changes in her office, primarily decorative. Corinne, the head of the administrative council, burst into the office and said, "You changed [this and that], and you didn't tell me!" Sheila, amazed, held back and stated, "The chair of the administrative council is not someone I have to report to when something is changed. I do appreciate all you have done, but there must be confusion about your role. The preacher is the head of the church, not the head of the council."

Then Fred, director of music, announced he was going to undergo another surgery. He had already been out for four or five weeks earlier in the year. Now he wanted additional paid leave. His estimated recovery time was two to three months. He planned to hire a string of soloists. Rev. Sheila reminded him of the personnel policy for part-time staff: three paid days of sick leave. As Rev. Sheila double-checked salary matters, she noticed the *former* administrative assistant had been slipping Fred a 5 percent raise on occasion.

Fred then suggested to Rev. Sheila that he place an ad in the church newsletter to poll the choir. Would they like to take off for the summer? At this point, Rev. Sheila stood her ground and reminded Fred that was not the choir's decision. According to standard church policy, a substitute would be hired at 35 percent of his salary while he received 65 percent. Fred tore up the ad for the church newsletter, slammed the door, and stormed out of the church. He called Rev. Sheila two days later and verbally attacked her.

Fred accused Rev. Sheila of trying to run his music program. Rev. Sheila reminded him of the details of his contract and mentioned items in the job description that he was neglecting. Fred retorted, "That's your fault; you didn't push me hard enough!"

Mike, the treasurer, heard of this exchange and was very upset. Behind Rev. Sheila's back, he announced to the chair of the finance committee, "We need to give Fred the money (i.e., his full salary while sick) and not tell Sheila."

A substitute director of music was hired, and the size of the choir doubled! Fred reappeared early from sick leave and announced his return. In passive-aggressive ways, he continued to undermine the pastor's authority.

A stampede was starting to form. Before we go further, can you spot the elephants? Remember that elephants in the church can be people, but they are also dynamics, relations, and issues. You may want to do this exercise in a small group format. Consider it a midterm in which you can share your insights.

Righteous Rumbling

Despite their extreme caution, elephants can find themselves in distress. To rescue a mired juvenile, a mother will run the risk of either meeting the same fate herself or having her weight cause an outcropping to collapse, hurtling her down a ravine to her death.[2]

The "righteous rumbling" at Moody Memorial UMC continued. Tension mounted. Accusations from Fred toward the pastor accelerated. The chair of parish staff relations, Dale, approached the pastor: "Reverend, Fred is livid. He has left us no alternative but to fire him." The district superintendent was called immediately, the bishop was notified, and a conclusion was unanimously reached. With these words, the director of music was fired: "Instead of working with the pastor, you have continued to go around her and made things worse. Staff parish has affirmed the decision. You are dismissed." Fred demanded vacation time, more sick leave, and other monetary concessions. When denied, he retorted, "I thought you were all my friends." His anger was directed totally at the pastor.

Dale notified Mike (the "patriarch of the church"), who became incensed. A chain of hostile events was set in place.

When Dale read the announcement of Fred's dismissal in a formal statement the next Sunday morning, a violent voice from within the congregation cried out as worship began: "It's not the music person; it's the preacher!" According to Rev. Sheila, it was as if the words "Crucify her, crucify her . . ." were an undercurrent in the outburst. She kept calm. At the time of the interview, she noted that some of those "acting out" that Sunday morning were persons with the disease of alcoholism. Had the series on the Twelve Steps of Alcoholics Anonymous added to this stampede?

Fred had a full-time business in town and began to organize his customers. A petition was written while Rev. Sheila was away on a one-week vacation. It was signed by twenty-five people, including one child. Upon returning, Rev. Sheila preached a sermon that ended with the words: "There is no place in Scripture that gives a person the right to destroy a church or a person."

Then the accusation began that Rev. Sheila was gay. Another rumor stated that she was going to remove the organ and put in a jazz band. Some of the senior members were afraid when they heard these rumors. One member tried to take her name off the petition when she realized the falsity of the allegations. This woman was not allowed to do so by the petition gatherers, primarily Fred and Corinne.

The finance committee had a regularly scheduled meeting. Fred's financial situation came up for discussion. Rev. Sheila announced, "What happened to Fred was his choice. It's over."

"NO, IT ISN'T!" screamed a committee member. The meeting got out of hand until Rev. Sheila calmly arose and turned off the lights. She adjourned the meeting. She was called names by some of the members as they exited the room. "You just didn't get your way," one said. Another said, "You have destroyed our sweet little church!" Some men continued to attack Rev. Sheila verbally. Rev. Sheila called the police for protection, concerned lest the trumpeting of threats escalated into physical assault.

The next day, Rev. Sheila commented to Cheryl, her faithful administrative aide, "Cheryl, this is so painful." Cheryl commented with the wisdom of one who has seen the inside of many churches: "Rev. Sheila, this isn't about you. It is about God making a church out of a social club."

Before I add the conclusion to this stampede, let us take an assessment of the elephants running loose in this church. Remember, sensitive issues in this church had been "untended" by Rev. Sheila's immediate predecessors. I asked Rev. Sheila for her list:

- Sexism: If a man is strong, he is a leader. If a woman is strong, she is an aggressor. Sheila actually used a word that means "female dog" (my publisher won't let me use it).

- Control: This church had a matriarch (Corinne), a patriarch (Mike), and a favored son (Fred). This "first family" was in control. They were in charge of administration, finances, and music.

- Church as a social club ("our sweet little church"): When Rev. Sheila first arrived, Fred tried to impress her with the fact that the leaders of the church were his best friends. As the new administrative assistant wisely noted, the church was functioning for those in control as a place to spend time with "best friends."

• Power dynamics: In this church, there was a triumvirate of power: matriarch—patriarch—favored son. In a way, a distinct triangle was formed, and the pastor was not a part of it.

• Discrimination (homophobia): The general attitude of the church was hostile to gays, or homophobic. When the accusation was made that Rev. Sheila was gay, this idea inflamed some of the people. At this time, the United Methodist Church does not allow for the ordination of gays and lesbians.

• Money: Money is power in the church. The chair of the finance committee, Mike, wielded considerable power and had a large say in matters of salary. Also, the dissidents in the church tried to exert power by withholding their pledges and tithes.

• Singleness: "When you are a single woman, some want to say you are sleeping around; others say you are gay. Parishioners cannot deal with the fact that you are single," said Rev. Sheila. In fact, Sheila was widowed. The traditional pastor has been male and often with a wife to assist him in house calls and other duties. The single male pastor makes some parishioners uncomfortable because his sexuality is not focused in a "monogamous marriage." He may still be "available" and therefore a sexual being! Theories as to his sexual orientation may also arise. All of these dynamics are even more pronounced for the single woman in ministry.

- Spiritual immaturity: At Moody Memorial, the United Methodist Women met at a Mexican restaurant at a bar so they could have their margaritas and chase those with a "quick devotional." Rev. Sheila had sensed a hunger and thirst for the Word of God when she was first introduced to the church and sought to reach this hunger and thirst with spiritual growth.

- Biblical illiteracy: One sixty-six-year-old member confessed that it was only with Rev. Sheila's coming that she had first started reading the Bible!

- Alcoholism: Rev. Sheila chose a sermon series that followed the Twelve Steps of Alcoholics Anonymous. As you may know, the first step is admitting one's powerlessness and helplessness over addiction. This series could be very uncomfortable to those in denial of their various addictions, including addictions to power, money, work, and status.

You may have seen different elephants running through the halls of the church. I have also wondered if ageism is one of them. It may be helpful to realize that fear is one of the reasons we tiptoe around elephants. Letty Russell, one of my seminary professors, taught me to ask myself, when confronted with defensiveness, rigidity, and controlling behavior in others, what would they have to lose if they gave up their view or position? This same question could be asked for each item in Sheila's list.

I was surprised to find a book titled *When Elephants Weep: The Emotional Lives of Animals.*[3] Based on scientific studies, field notes, anecdotal stories, ethnology, observations of animal behaviorists, and animal trainers, the book demonstrates that animals display a wide range of emotions that are deeply felt. We know that animals experience fear, but scientists are revealing how animals communicate fear. In Hwange National Park, Zimbabwe, elephants are culled each year. Culling is the selective removal of animals, on occasion through killing. Sometimes this has to do with disease, sometimes with overpopulation, sometimes for monetary gain.

In Hwange National Park, "during this culling, elephant family groups are herded by aircraft toward hunters who shoot all except the young calves, who are rounded up for sale. The elephant calves run around, scream, and search for their mothers. One year a wildlife guide at a private sanctuary ninety miles away from the park noticed that eighty elephants vanished from their usual haunts on the day the culling started at Hwange."[4] Several days later, he found them bunched together at the other end of the sanctuary, as far away from the park as they were able to go. Elephants communicate through subsonic call, which is sound pitched too low for people to hear. In the Hwange case, sanctuary elephants received subsonic sounds from the frightened Hwange elephants. This is not to say that the sanctuary elephants knew the exact nature of the threat. Rather, they knew there was a threat to their way of life: "The object of their fear was inchoate, but the fear was real."[5]

The Sweet Little Church Revisited

The stampede began to die down in Moody Memorial UMC. The malcontents withheld their pledges (money), hoping that this shortfall of funds would drive Rev. Sheila away. One senior citizen came within two inches of Sheila's face and said, "You're the biggest disappointment of my life." He had been told Sheila was gay.

The district superintendent stood by Sheila, as did other loyal church members. At one of the first sermons after the dust of discord was settling, Sheila began to clear the air: "I have been so focused on the storm of dust and dirt, I may have missed the Savior. God is doing a new thing in this church." Applause broke out in the sanctuary. Sheila picked up Fred's Sunday School class, which he had taught for sixteen years; no one left. Sheila gave me a prayer from Rabbi Harold Kushner which begins:

> Let the rain come and wash away
> the ancient grudges, the bitter hatreds.[6]

Hannibal and the Elephants

Hannibal wanted to conquer Rome, but he never did. What he is famous for is his march across the Alps with thirty-seven elephants in 318 BC. Everyone thought his plan was absurd; Hannibal was especially ridiculed by his three brothers, Hasdrubal, Hanno, and Mago.[7]

As a young boy in Carthage, on an outing with his family, Hannibal witnessed a herd of elephants fighting. His mother remarked that those elephants reminded her of her sons. Hannibal started thinking. When he saw that a baby elephant was left behind, he asked permission to take him home. His father agreed. When his father later left for Spain, Hannibal and his elephant went along. Hannibal knew of the strength of elephants. Eventually, he arranged for thirty-six elephants to be shipped from Carthage to Spain. His brothers came with the shipments of elephants. They watched him train these elephants over a period of a year. Hannibal capitalized on the strength and endurance of the elephants.

Hannibal met many challenges, including crossing the Rhone River. This required building a stationary platform, then two giant rafts covered in mud and grass. The elephants were led onto the rafts, and they weren't afraid. They thought they were on the ground! Some elephants actually tried the water and liked it. All thirty-seven elephants made it across the Rhone River. Eventually, with much effort, the caravan made it through the Alps into Italy. Although Hannibal did not conquer Rome, he organized and tamed the elephants. Rev. Sheila's journey is no less remarkable. Are there any ways you have handled such a situation or would handle it differently?

Chapter Four

The Elephant That Crushes Your Spirit: Depression

When upon life's billows you are tempest tossed,
When you are discouraged thinking all is lost,
Count your many blessings, name them one by one,
And it will surprise you what the Lord hath done.

Are you ever burdened with a load of care?
Does the cross seem heavy you are called to bear?
Count your many blessings, ev'ry doubt will fly,
And you will be singing as the days go by.

So, amid the conflict, whether great or small,
Do not be discouraged, God is over all;
Count your many blessings, angels will attend,
Help and comfort give you to your journey's end.

Count your blessings, name them one by one;
Count your blessings, see what God hath done;

Count your blessings, name them one by one;
Count your many blessings, see what God hath done.
—Johnson Oatman Jr., 1897

This chapter is about the dangers of depression, and, frankly, in this case the image of a dragon works better. The final verse of Leonard Lipton and Peter Yarrow's "Puff the Magic Dragon" describes Puff's sadness when the boy Jackie Paper grows up and no longer comes to play. The major portion of the song describes a child and the creations of his imagination, the simple joys and enchantment of youthful play and creativity. At the end of that folk ballad, Puff the Magic Dragon bends his head and sheds his green scales in sadness, stops his visits to Cherry Lane, and retreats to his cave in sorrow at the loss of his young human friend. Jackie is growing up and doesn't have room for dragons, "strings and sealing wax and other fancy stuff."[1]

Whether one calls it an elephant, a dragon, or another beast, depression is an under-recognized, under-diagnosed, and under-treated disorder that afflicts many people. A communiqué issued by the Centers for Disease Control and Prevention (the CDC) in anticipation of the 2010 National Depression Screening Day named depression as the third leading cause of disease burden worldwide, meaning depression is responsible for significant health care expenditures, lost work days and wages, related health problems, and deaths. The CDC predicted that by 2020 depression would be surpassed only by cardiovascular disease in the various categories of disease burden. In recent surveys, at least 9 percent of adults in the United States reported symptoms of depression in the two weeks immediately before they were queried.[2] Given the sheer number of individuals affected by depression, the stresses of caregiving inherent to ministry, the expectations to be "perfect in pulpit and parish," and the stigma of mental illness in general, depression is one of the biggest elephants in any room of clergy and church professionals.

I grew up in church and the Sam Seminarian and Pamela Pastor[3] American church culture with its numerous and predictable customs, rituals, and programs, including Sunday night youth groups, vacation Bible school, church camps, and regional denominational organizations. I met several Sams and Pamelas as a teen and younger layperson. I later became reacquainted with them in seminary and professional circles as I became a clergywoman, and I have cared for them for more than twenty years as a physician and psychiatrist. While all Sams and Pamelas are individuals with unique aspects of their personal and professional lives, their stories share common concerns and themes with those of many other students and professionals in ministry.

***

Sam was referred to me by his seminary. A youthful-looking, single, thirty-five-year-old man, he was encouraged to consider ordained ministry by a high-ranking denominational official after managing a regional youth camping program for seven years. An engaging, personable young man, he shared with me that he had taken seven years to complete his undergraduate degree, switching majors several times, finally squeaking through to earn a bachelor's degree in general studies. Having grown up in the church, he had considered his camp manager position to be his dream job—free room and board at a financially well-endowed camp property, minimal if any responsibilities during a long off-season, and few stresses or demands during the summer camp season. He served at the pleasure of his denominational official, who remained happy as long as Sam's winsome, magnetic personality translated into high ratings and return commitments from camp constituencies. When the denomination began its initiative to encourage younger adults to consider ministry, Sam was enthusiastically endorsed to the Commission on Ministry by clergy and laity alike.

Despite glowing letters of recommendation for his seminary application, Sam struggled academically his first semester. He dropped two classes mid-term and barely passed his remaining courses. He took half a load second term, remaining on academic probation. He became socially withdrawn, slept twelve to fourteen hours a day, and felt uncharacteristically sad. In addition, he had difficulty concentrating and making even simple decisions, and he neglected his personal care and hygiene. He started drinking heavily, his self-esteem plummeted, and he avoided all contact with seminary and denominational officials. The school's referral to a psychiatrist was prompted by a desperate call from a denominational official to seminary leadership, demanding to know what was going on with their beloved Sam.

During Sam's first appointment with me, he readily agreed with all the facts that brought him to my office. In addition, he confided that he had gained more than thirty pounds since seminary enrollment, felt guilty about letting down people in his church and hopeless about his prospects of finishing seminary and entering ordained ministry. He reported he had not had any thoughts of suicide, but he knew he was becoming more and more depressed:

For years, all I heard were Bible verses like "Rejoice in the Lord always; again I will say, Rejoice" and "the fruit of the Spirit is love, joy, peace, patience, kindness, generosity, faithfulness, gentleness, and self-control."[4] These just aren't working for me here. I guess I expected seminary to be more like a church camp for grown-ups, complete with "Kum Ba Yah" and "Pass It On" every night. No one told me it's really graduate school!

***

Pamela Pastor is a fifty-five-year-old woman serving a mid-sized church in a town of about five thousand residents. She married at twenty-two, immediately after earning an education degree, and had three children by the age of thirty. Her husband traveled a great deal, and the marriage ended when her children were in elementary school. She credits her church at that time for being her "life-line and beacon of hope." She became increasingly active in the religious education and mission programs, then enrolled in a seminary one hundred miles away when her youngest child entered high school. Her mother helped with the children three days and nights a week for three years so Pamela could complete her MDiv. Since ordination, she has served the same church in an adjacent town, a thirty-mile round trip from the home she has lived in for thirty-three years. Since her youngest child completed college a few years ago, Pamela reports a waning enthusiasm for ministry, diminished energy, disrupted sleep, weight gain, frequent crying spells, anxiety that seems to come out of nowhere, indecisiveness, and lack of interest in activities that have always interested her and given her pleasure. She is slow to return telephone calls to family and friends and often locks her office door at church and puts her head on her desk for hours at a time instead of attending to church business.

Pamela is recycling old sermons or taking them from on-line sermon mills, both practices she promised herself she would never do. She has not cleaned her house in ages, and she does not get out of bed unless she has to go in to church. She had dreamed of remarrying someday, but she feels hopeless about meeting a suitable single man in her small town. She has thoughts of being better off dead than trapped in her current life, but she says she would never harm herself because she would devastate her children if she committed suicide. Fearful that senior church leaders were suspecting her job performance was slipping, Pamela Pastor called a psychiatrist for help before her depression worsened beyond its current severity and she lost her position. At her first appointment, she said, "You know, my parents raised me on 'Count Your Blessings,' 'Love Lifted Me,' and 'In My Heart There Rings a Melody' theology. But sometimes when you're blue, gospel songs and prayer can use some help!"

Depression: The Elephant That Sits on You

Depression is a very common elephant in the lives of seminarians, clergy, church musicians, and other church staff of all varieties. In some instances, experiencing and surviving a depressive episode are a part of one's personal history and development that nurtures one's gifts and graces for pastoral ministry—for listening to the spoken and unspoken needs of others, for recognizing pain and suffering, and for understanding the role of Christians as God's ears and hands in earthly caregiving. Depression can be found hand in hand with spiritual doubts and angst in "dark nights of the soul," together igniting spiritual awakenings and yearnings for greater intimacy and a closer walk with God. For the most part, however, when one is in the throes of depression, there is nothing romantic or inspiring about it at all. You can read about the fruit of the Spirit, about rejoicing in the Lord, and recall all the feel-good gospel hymns, and though they may help some, you wind up feeling more worthless—even more sinful—when these approaches to lifting your mood do not work.

Depression can feel like the largest elephant in the *Guinness Book of World Records* has plopped down on your chest, preventing you from drawing your next breath, crushing your spirit along with all your bones, gagging you with the foul odor of a reeking pachyderm, totally helpless and paralyzed. And if the depression is really severe, you might not even care. This predicament is magnified and has indeterminable ripple effects on countless others when the depressed person is the minister.

What Is Depression?

Depression is a complex collection of mood symptoms with medical, biological, physiological, and/or genetic elements contributing to its risk factors, onset, exacerbation, and treatments. Psychological factors are equally important to consider in its origin, risk factors, and treatment. Spiritual considerations are the third major area to consider when thinking about what is contributing to depression, and even more important to invoke in treatment as sources of comfort, coping, and healing. While the verses of the old gospel hymn "Count Your Blessings" were penned long before the biological and psychological underpinnings of mood disorders were recognized and appreciated, both the medical field and religious professionals must guard against swinging so far into the directions of neurobiology and psychology that the timeless truths, comforts, and strengths of faith are either ignored or under-nurtured in ourselves and those for whom we care about and pastor.

The bottom line is that no matter the biopsychosocial, religious, and spiritual factors contributing to or complicating one's individual depressive episode, depression is not just any common elephant—it often feels more like a huge herd of woolly mammoths! Now that we have named it, let's talk about it, try to understand it, and learn where to turn for help in treating and managing it.

As we continue, remember that the sole purpose of this chapter is to share general information about depression and its treatment, thereby raising awareness about this disorder in its intended audience. Readers concerned that they or someone else they know or care about might be depressed should consult their own psychiatrists or other qualified clinicians for appropriate diagnosis and treatment of all health concerns.

What Are the Signs and Symptoms of Depression?

Depression is one of several mood disorders recognized by the American Psychiatric Association in the *Diagnostic and Statistical Manual of Mental Disorders, Fourth Edition, Text Revision* (DSM-IV-TR).[5] Signs and symptoms may include the following:

- Depressed or sad mood most of the day, nearly every day; may include excessive or uncharacteristic tearfulness

- Loss of interest or pleasure in usual or enjoyable activities; often includes decreased interest in sexual activity

- Increased or decreased appetite; may have significant weight gain or weight loss

- Sleep difficulties, which may include difficulty falling asleep, early morning awakening, or excessive sleepiness

- Restlessness, irritability, agitation

- Fatigue, decreased energy, slowness of movements, or feeling slowed down

- Feelings of helplessness, hopelessness, or worthlessness

- Thoughts that you or others would be better off if you were dead, thoughts of killing yourself, or actual suicide plans or attempts

While DSM-IV-TR requires other duration and exclusionary criteria be met for the diagnosis of a major depressive episode and disorder, it emphasizes that the symptoms cause noticeable distress and/or impairment in the depressed person's occupational and social functioning—meaning interpersonal relationships.

Since I started my psychiatry training more than two decades ago, the specialty has gone through three different versions of the DSM. The field has been planning for DSM-V for several years now, and we anticipate its finished form to be ready for use in 2013. While the DSM is certainly the ultimate in diagnostic art and science, the purpose of this chapter is not to focus on minute details, beginning and ending dates of particular symptoms, the exact number of symptoms expressed, or even rating scales of depression severity. While all of this information is necessary and can be very helpful in the diagnostic and treatment process, when I work appointment by appointment or session by session with depressed clergy, I find it most productive and useful to focus on the particular symptoms of depression that are most distressing in their individual personal, professional and spiritual lives. For instance, someone with "only" three concerns—sad mood, excessive fatigue, and inability to concentrate and make decisions—may be just as stymied by these symptoms as another person who endorses five or more symptoms. In other words, I have found it helpful to consider depression as a family of illnesses. Every individual's depression is unique to him or her, and the particular symptoms can also be considered the targets of treatment and the mileposts by which to measure improvement.

Are There Different Kinds of Depressive Disorders?

The terminology used by professionals and the plethora of ways depression is referred to in the media can be very confusing and often contradictory. While in this chapter I am using the term *depression* in a very general way to indicate a collection of physical and emotional symptoms causing personal, professional, and/or spiritual distress and meriting treatment, clergy and seminarians should be familiar with terms for specific forms of depression they may hear about as they minister in their congregations. A *major depressive episode* refers to two weeks of depressed mood or loss of interest or pleasure in usual activities, plus five or more of the symptoms mentioned earlier in this chapter. A *major depressive disorder* typically is diagnosed after one or more major depressive episodes that are not complicated by mania or psychotic disorders. The terms *major depressive episode* and *major depressive disorder* often are used interchangeably.

Do you know parishioners who are chronically unhappy, always seem to have a couple of depressive symptoms lingering around, yet still manage to hold down a job and come to church nearly every Sunday, but whose irritable, negative mood always casts a bit of a pall over vestry, session, or deacon meetings? They might have *dysthymic disorder*, or a chronic, low-grade depressive disorder typically not as severe or acute as a major depressive episode. If someone has major depressive episodes *and* manic episodes (elevated or irritable mood, grandiosity, decreased need for sleep, increased rate of thoughts and/or speech, increased risk-taking or pleasure-seeking), he or she may have a form of *bipolar disorder*, often referred to by the historic name of *manic-depressive illness*. *Cyclothymic disorder* is a chronic, usually less pronounced and often less severe form of bipolar disorder. When a woman becomes severely depressed within four weeks of delivering a baby, the specifier *postpartum onset* can be added to the diagnosis. The specifier *seasonal pattern* may be applied when a pattern of depressive symptoms occurs at one time of the year, often late fall or winter, and regularly remits at other times of year, usually spring or summer. Other forms of depression are caused or exacerbated by substance abuse or dependence, medical conditions, and side effects of a number of prescription medications.[6] We will talk about these shortly.

What Causes Depression?

Research into the causes of depression is ongoing and encompasses genetics, neurochemistry and other biological factors, environmental and toxic causes, structural anomalies, or variations of the brain anatomy and physiology. Many brain imaging and other medical studies have identified differences in the way brain cells communicate with each other via neurotransmitters and how parts of the brain dealing with sleep, appetite, mood, and thought processing work differently in depressed individuals than in people who are not depressed. Hormones and their related functions throughout the body, not just in brain structures, are hypothesized to have roles in mood disorders, including protective effects. The immune system and its influence on psychiatric illness is a new frontier for study, as are changes that can occur within single brain cells during insult or injury and cumulatively over a lifetime.[7]

In addition, studies of psychological and sociological determinants or influences in mood disorders are ongoing at many research centers. These include paradigms for understanding depression offered by the various schools of psychological theory, such as psychoanalysis, attachment theory, behavior theory, object relations, and family theory, to name a few. Social, societal, and cultural contributors to mood disorders are also important factors in illness expression. The presence of war, a bad economy, high unemployment rates, homelessness, stresses such as being the primary caregiver for a relative with Alzheimer's disease, and exposure to violence and trauma may contribute to or exacerbate depressive symptoms.[8] While many clergy can point out the cumulative toll of these stresses to their congregants, as a group we are not particularly good at recognizing these elephants in our own lives that may contribute to our own depressive symptoms.

Instead of focusing on concrete causes of depression, I have found thinking in terms of *risk factors* to be more helpful in identifying symptoms as they occur, making the actual diagnosis, and—most important—raising awareness about depression and educating clergy and laity alike about treatments, ongoing monitoring, and adaptive changes that can be made even without a physician's prescription. Significant risk factors for depression include a previous mood disorder (depression tends to be a recurrent illness, especially when untreated or inadequately treated), recent significant losses such as a close family death or loss of job and livelihood, and a family history of a mood disorder. Other risk factors are substance abuse, medical issues, chronic pain, break-up of marriages or other close romantic relationships, unmarried status and/or or living alone, and lower socioeconomic status. As mentioned before, exposure to trauma is a risk factor for depression, whether individual, such as from a rape or a horrible car accident, or a mass trauma, such as being affected by large wildfires that have burned in many regions of the United States in recent years.[9]

Does Age Make a Difference?

In the last decade, we have learned that children and adolescents experience depression at rates greater than previously thought. Most studies of adult depression, however, have found the average age of onset to be between twenty-seven and thirty years of age. Older adults often experience additional risk factors for depression with loss of spouse, failing physical health, and blows to their identity, self-esteem, or perceived life purpose if they are not ready for retirement or not fully prepared for the inherent changes it brings.[10] Many senior clergy are still serving into their advanced years, by either choice or necessity, and can be found in full-time, very intense positions, as well as part-time, interim, and volunteer ministries. In the general population, most seniors are generally doing well and are not particularly predisposed to depression, especially in the absence of severe medical problems. When elderly adults do become depressed, they may not complain spontaneously about being depressed.[11] They tend to lose weight more often than gain, have problems with insomnia more than sleeping too much, experience loss of pleasure in usual activities, and have issues with impaired concentration and memory.[12] In my experience, the presence of a depressed older clergyperson, either as a church member or on staff, can be a huge elephant in the church. Parishioners, clergy colleagues, and even family members and friends tiptoe around the issue, worried that their concern about the individual's mental health will be misunderstood as lack of appreciation for years of experience and service, an effort to push the minister into retirement, an "accusation" that dementia has set in, or a combination of all three.

Are There Gender Differences?

Women are at greater risk than men to develop depression, though overall men and women are at equal risk for developing other psychiatric disorders. A combination of hormonal fluctuations over the life cycle and perhaps a stronger genetic predisposition to depression than men may account for more depressive illnesses in women. Before puberty, the incidence of depression in males and females is roughly equivalent; then girls are diagnosed with the disorder at greater rates than boys as adolescence progresses. Rates of depression in women increase again after menopause. In terms of psychosocial stresses, men tend to become depressed due to occupational stresses, whereas women are more troubled by close interpersonal relationship difficulties.[13] Women commonly demonstrate more symptoms of sadness, worthlessness, and excessive guilt, while men are more likely to be tired, irritable, experience sleep troubles, and lose interest in activities that they usually enjoy. Depressed men may also turn to alcohol and drugs more often than depressed women.[14]

The gender elephant is a particularly cantankerous beast when dealing with depressed clergy, particularly females. The depressed clergywoman is often loath to admit it, lest she be misunderstood as being too emotional, not able to handle the stresses of ministry, or unable to do the job as well as a man. Similarly, church members and congregational and denominational authorities may not recognize that the manifestations of "female temperament" may be true biological depression. Another worry is that they might be accused of gender discrimination for insisting that a woman seek help for depression, especially if male peers are not treated in a similar fashion when they suffer from psychiatric illness. On the other hand, our male clergy and churches may see depression as a weakness, despite the significant progress that has been made subduing the stigma mammoth. Bottom line: no one enjoys wrestling with the depression elephant, male or female!

What Other Illnesses Can Accompany Depression?

Depression often coexists with other distinct psychiatric disorders. It is important that these be identified and appropriately treated as well, lest all existing conditions complicate treatment and contribute to a poorer outcome. Anxiety disorders are the group of disorders diagnosed most frequently with depression and include phobias or fears, panic, generalized anxiety, post-traumatic stress, and obsessive-compulsive disorders. Substance use, eating disorders, and personality disorders are often comorbid with depression, and depression and dementia may both be present in the elderly.[15]

Medical conditions can increase the rates and severity of depression. Illnesses known to be associated with a significant prevalence of depression include cancer, diabetes, heart disease, chronic obstructive pulmonary disease, asthma, HIV/AIDS, stroke, epilepsy, multiple sclerosis, and Parkinson's disease. In addition, several medications used in general medical practice have been linked to possible depressive symptoms.[16]

Like people, elephants sometimes travel in pairs and larger groups. After one identifies the first elephant, be aware that their buddies, other psychiatric illnesses and medical conditions, might be lurking around as well, making the depression worse or more difficult to treat.

How is Depression Diagnosed?

Depression is chiefly what is called a "clinical diagnosis." This means that in most cases a physician or mental health clinician takes a thorough history from the individual and, with permission, from significant others. Thorough past psychiatric and medical histories, including substance abuse, and educational, military, vocational, family, and legal histories are important to know. Current marital status, family, and living situations are also important to understand. In addition, I like to inquire about strengths, talents, personal disappointments, greatest moments, and future dreams and aspirations. If available, records from clinicians treating past depressions or other concerns should be reviewed. The clinician should meet in person with the patient or client to assess current mood, how well he or she appears to be processing thoughts, the presence of additional anxiety or psychotic symptoms, and to listen to any accompanying concerns. Several questionnaires and self-report scales have been developed to assist with the diagnosis of depression, its severity, the risk of committing suicide, quality of life during treatment, and the overall success of treatment. Many clinicians find these tools helpful in the diagnostic and treatment processes.

Often psychiatrists and primary care clinicians will request or perform physical examinations, looking for those coexisting medical concerns mentioned earlier. Various laboratory tests may be obtained as well. Examples include studies to check for anemia or thyroid issues as causes or contributors to fatigue and loss of energy. Remember that several signs of depression—such as fatigue, low energy, and sleep and appetite changes—also are found in many physical conditions. In addition, one of the best treatments for depression is taking good care of the rest of your body!

What Treatments Are Available for Depression?

The first step in treating depression may not seem much like a "treatment," but for serious depressions with the risk of suicide, it is arguably the most important. This is to establish the proper setting for immediate treatment. If someone is harmful to self or others, or has psychotic symptoms (hallucinations, delusions, or paranoia) along with depressive symptoms, the most appropriate treatment setting is typically an inpatient psychiatry unit. This setting is designed with the safety of patients and staff in mind, and often intensive treatment can be accomplished more quickly with the higher level of professional attention and monitoring. After stabilization is achieved, less restrictive settings for care can be considered, such as partial hospitalization (a few to several hours three to five days a week and the patient sleeps at home) or regular outpatient care.

When the public thinks about treatment for depression these days, the first thing that pops into mind has to be antidepressant medications. As a physician, psychiatrist, clergywoman, and mother, I believe that the best antidepressant is none if medication truly is not indicated. On the other hand, I think it is at least equally ill-advised not to avail oneself of a treatment that can improve one's quality of life and one's ability to serve God, the church, and others in ministry. This is especially the case in instances of severe depression, for which antidepressants can be lifesaving.

Generic names for commonly prescribed antidepressants today include fluoxetine, citalopram, escitalopram, sertraline, bupropion, venlafaxine, desvenlafaxine, duloxetine, and mirtazapine, among others. Some individuals still benefit from older classes of medications, including tricyclic antidepressants and monoamine oxidase inhibitors.[17] The goal here is not an exhaustive chapter on antidepressants. It is the prescribing physician's job to recommend specific treatments based on the presentation, possible coexisting psychiatric and medical conditions, the gender and age of the depressed individual, and family history and treatment responses. I never make final recommendations without considering insurance and the patient's financial situation, and discussing these matters candidly if they are likely to affect the course and success of any treatment. Before pastors accept a prescription for any medication, especially antidepressants, they should insist that the physician review why a specific agent is being recommended and the benefits and risks of that medicine—in theological terms, I call these the potential "blessings and burdens" of the antidepressant. The doctor should also discuss what alternative medications exist and why they are not being recommended first, the risk/benefit ratio of no medication at all, the dose that will be started and how quickly it will be increased, and how closely the clinician needs to monitor the individual once medication treatment is initiated. Other important items to ask about are possible interactions with medications the pastor is taking for other medical or psychiatric conditions, the names and doses of over-the-counter and herbal medicines she or he is taking, and the pros and cons of generic formulations of the antidepressant. All of this information constitutes the process of *informed consent.* Also, be sure to get phone numbers and other twenty-four-hour contact information for the prescribing physician and those who share call and cross-coverage responsibilities during nights, weekends, holidays, and other non-office hour times.

Clergy often ask me about the *black box warnings* for antidepressants. In addition to wanting to know for their own care, many have said that parents of teens and young adults in their churches who are taking antidepressants have mentioned this as a concern. Black box warnings in general are warnings or alerts placed on medications by the U.S. Food and Drug Administration (FDA) when there are concerns about the safety of those medications. These concerns can pertain to certain patient populations involved, the condition(s) being treated, or life-threatening or serious short- or long-term side effects. In 2003, a possible association between suicidal thinking and the antidepressant paroxetine was noticed in controlled treatment trials in children and adolescents.[18] This prompted the FDA to ask all manufacturers of antidepressants to resubmit safety data from pediatric studies for additional analysis. That analysis of twenty-four pediatric antidepressant trials revealed a 4 percent risk of suicidality in youth on active medication and a 2 percent risk of the same in study subjects receiving a placebo, or inactive drug. Based on that analysis, in 2004 the FDA issued a black box warning for all antidepressant use in children and adolescents. Along with the warning, guidelines were issued recommending patient monitoring consisting of weekly in-person, face-to-face visits with the prescribing clinician for four weeks, followed by biweekly check-ups for the next four-week period, and then monthly appointments.[19] A subsequent analysis of 295 placebo-controlled trials involving approximately 77,000 subjects found a similar increased risk of suicidal ideation in young adults up to the age of twenty-four years. Consequently, in December 2006 the FDA extended the black box warnings for antidepressants for individuals up to twenty-four years old.[20]

As you might predict, both the number of people diagnosed with depression and the number of antidepressant prescriptions written in these age groups decreased after the black box warnings were issued.[21] Furthermore, the decrease in antidepressant prescriptions has been correlated to an increased number of completed suicides in the years right after issuance of the black box warnings.[22] This issue primarily affects younger seminarians who are depressed and are considering antidepressant therapy. The risk of suicide in untreated individuals can be substantial. The critical factor for not only reducing suicide risk when taking an antidepressant, but also for providing optimal care and achieving the best possible treatment outcome in general, is regular and consistent face-to-face follow-up appointments with the prescribing physician at the intervals the doctor instructs given the field's best evidence-based treatment guidelines and recommendations. In other words, even studying, writing papers, exams, and your supervised ministry placements must not prevent you from missing your appropriate and necessary follow-up appointments with your psychiatrist!

Another common treatment for depression is *psychotherapy*, sometimes referred to as "talk therapy." Depending on the individual patient or client and the biological, psychological, medical, and other factors contributing to the depressive episode, depression sometimes can be treated by psychotherapy alone, but often the best treatment results occur with a combination of psychotherapy and antidepressant therapy. Common forms, or schools, of psychotherapy for depression used by professionals today include insight-oriented psychodynamic psychotherapy, cognitive and behavioral therapies, interpersonal therapy, problem-solving therapy, group therapy, and—when indicated based on the individual's specific situation—marital and family therapies. Studies especially support the effectiveness of cognitive-behavioral, interpersonal, and behavioral therapies.[23] Clergy seeking treatment for depression should work with their prescribing physicians and psychotherapists regarding the psychotherapeutic treatment modalities for their personal needs.

There are additional forms of treatment for depression that has not responded as well as desired to medication and/or psychotherapy, or for individuals for whom treatment with antidepressant medications might be contraindicated. I believe these are worth mentioning, if for no other reason than that readers will hear about them in the media, and in their ministries pastors will have parishioners receiving these treatments. *Electroconvulsive therapy*, or ECT, has an unfavorable reputation in many public circles, largely due to stigma, bad jokes, and its portrayal in movies. However, it can be lifesaving and is an excellent treatment for some very severe forms of depression when performed by well-trained psychiatrists working with experienced anesthesiologists and medical teams in accredited medical settings. *Vagus nerve stimulation* (VNS) has been approved by the United States Food and Drug Administration (FDA) for treatment-resistant depression. *Transcranial magnetic stimulation* (TMS) is another, newer treatment modality that shows promise in ongoing clinical trials. Much more established, less controversial, and in general use for many years is *light therapy*, an accepted and effective treatment for the depressive component of seasonal affective disorder.[24]

You've Mentioned "Suicide." What Should I Know about Depression as It Relates to Suicide?

One way to think of suicide is as the worst outcome of untreated, under-treated, or treatment-resistant depression. It is a significant public health problem and is not totally unique to depression. In a recent year for which reliable statistical analysis has been documented, suicide was the tenth leading cause of death in the United States, claiming almost 35,000 lives. American Indian and Alaska natives and non-Hispanic whites, especially non-Hispanic white men age eighty-five and older, have higher suicide rates than other ethnic groups. Risk factors for suicide include the following:

- Depression or other psychiatric disorders

- Substance use disorders

- Previous suicide attempts

- Family history of suicide, mental illness, or substance abuse

- Physical or sexual abuse

- Family violence

- Access to firearms

- Incarceration[25]

Other factors to consider when assessing suicide risk are the presence of hopelessness or decreased self-esteem, severe anxiety or panic attacks, psychosis, or recent psychiatric hospitalization. Chronic medical illness is a well-known risk factor, especially if it is disabling, is accompanied by chronic pain, or has a poor prognosis. Interpersonal losses, estrangement from family members, living alone, financial difficulties, and a history of childhood traumas, such as physical or sexual abuse, are additional risk factors for suicide. Protective factors against suicide include children in the home, a sense of family responsibility, and certain religious and cultural beliefs.[26]

What if I Know Someone Who Is Suicidal?

A common myth in the general public is that asking people if they are thinking of or planning on killing themselves is going to plant that idea in their minds and actually cause them to do it. This is just not true! The best way to find out if someone is thinking about harming himself or herself is to ask directly, "Are you thinking about hurting or killing yourself? Do you have a plan?" If you are suicidal or know of someone who is or might be, it is important to obtain immediate help. If at all possible, the suicidal person should not be alone and should not have access to weapons or medications that can be ingested in overdose. He or she should be seen by a qualified professional as soon as possible, whether it be the clinician already involved in his or her care, a walk-in clinic at the local community health center, or the nearest emergency room. Calling 911 is always an option, too. The suicidal individual or another on his behalf can call the National Suicide Prevention Lifeline at 1-800-273-TALK (8255). This number is available twenty-four hours a day, every day, and is toll free.[27]

In my professional clergy life, I have served with or known several ministers who have killed themselves. A few had known risk factors, and others were struggling, but few, if any, of their peers, family members, or parishioners knew or appreciated the degree of their suffering. All whose lives touched or were touched by those ministers were affected profoundly, not only by their deaths, but by the way they died. Our leaders in theological education, the institutional church, and many denominations must be applauded for the work they have done and what they have accomplished in the last few decades regarding clergy care, depression, and suicide awareness. But when it makes an appearance, the clergy suicide elephant is one of the biggest out there, and one of the most difficult to talk about and deal with because it is so painful for all involved.

Who Treats Depression, What Do They Do, and How Do I Assess Their Qualifications?

Psychiatrists are physicians, or MDs, who specialize in the diagnosis and treatment of psychiatric disorders. Psychiatric disorders commonly are called mental, emotional, and behavioral disorders. Psychiatrists have graduated from college, had four years of medical school, one year of internship, which includes several months of primary care and neurology, with at least three additional years of psychiatric residency training. If those requirements have been completed, they are eligible to take written and oral examinations and earn specialty board certification through the American Board of Psychiatry and Neurology (ABPN). Many psychiatrists go through additional years of subspecialty training in child and adolescent, addiction, forensic, geriatric psychiatry, and psychosomatic medicine (the psychiatric subspecialty that focuses on caring for the psychiatric needs of the medically ill). In recent years, the ABPN has adopted rigorous requirements for recertification every ten years. The ABPN website is a great place to learn more about psychiatry and its subspecialties: www.abpn.com. It also has a search function that permits viewing the certification status of individual psychiatrists.[28] While accredited psychiatry residency training programs are mandated to teach psychotherapy and some psychiatrists do offer psychotherapy themselves, the reality of the modern health care marketplace and the need for those with medical training to apply it to prescription practices means that many psychiatric physicians concentrate on initial assessments, medication monitoring, and leadership of multidisciplinary treatment teams. What clergy commonly will find is that the psychiatrist will prescribe and monitor antidepressant medication and work collaboratively with other therapists and clinicians involved in one's care.

Family practice and *internal medicine physicians,* some *neurologists,* and *nurse practitioners* often prescribe antidepressants. Whether and how much they prescribe depends on their training in this area, their personal comfort level with this class of medications, the availability of psychiatrists in the communities they serve, and how busy their practices are, among other factors.

Psychologists are a heterogeneous group of professionals who study and practice psychotherapy, behavioral therapy, psychological and educational assessment, psychoeducation, and research. They practice in private groups, community mental health centers, schools, inpatient and outpatient settings, residential settings, and county agencies. They may have master's degrees, PhDs, or doctor of psychology (PsyD) degrees. Licensure is granted by states. Usually, internships and/or residencies approved by accrediting bodies and significant hours of patient contact and supervision are required for licensure. The American Psychological Association is psychology's primary professional organization, with more than 154,000 members. Clergy benefit from the individual psychotherapies, behavioral therapies, marital and group therapies, and specialized addictions and vocational assessments offered by psychologists.[29]

Social workers are also helpful to many depressed clergy and seminarians. They are also licensed by the states and have master's degrees (MSW, MSSA), though academics and those in leadership positions will have PhDs or the Doctor of Social Work (DSW) degree. Social workers have diverse job descriptions, including individual psychotherapy, group therapy, abuse work, patient advocacy, and interfacing with services in the community needed by clergy and their families. They may be found in private practices, community mental health centers, hospitals, medical offices, and county offices and agencies. The National Association of Social Workers has more than 145,000 members and is headquartered in Washington, D.C. Its website contains information useful to ministers both personally and professionally.[30]

It may seem redundant to review what pastoral counselors have to offer to depressed ministers, but I have encountered many pastors in parish ministry and many seminarians whose professional and personal journeys have not afforded them contact with the pastoral care world. *Pastoral counselors* or *pastoral psychotherapists* are quite a diverse group. Their education and training range from no formal psychological training to second-career clergy who may have been mental health professionals during their previous working lives. They may counsel individuals in their congregations as part of their pastoral responsibilities or work in churches, synagogues, private practices, or larger pastoral care centers as full-time psychotherapists. Pastoral counselors vary regarding how much religious and spiritual content they bring into or encourage in therapy sessions. The most reputable professional guild for pastoral counselors is the American Association of Pastoral Counselors (AAPC). AAPC certification requires a three-year professional seminary degree, a master's or doctoral degree or equivalent mental health education within a training program, approximately 1,400 hours of supervised clinical experience, and 250 contact hours of direct supervision by approved supervisors.[31]

For depressed clergy and seminarians, psychotherapy with a qualified pastoral psychotherapist has the advantages of general shared backgrounds and experiences that permit the therapist greater insight into some of the patient's or client's struggles. On the other hand, like all care providers, the therapist must be well-trained and seasoned enough not to make inaccurate assumptions about or over-identify with his or her depressed pastor-patient.

Finally, *marriage and family therapists* are another group of professionals who work with depressed religious professionals. This is the most diverse group of clinicians, consisting of psychologists, social workers, educators, nurses, and others who identify themselves based on the services they provide and the client or patient population they serve, instead of their discipline of origin. Certification is granted by individual states, though there is considerable variability of standards from state to state. Typically, at least two years of clinical supervision is required for certification. The American Association for Marriage and Family Therapy also conducts a national examination.[32]

What Other Words of Advice Might Be Helpful?

This section is, in medicine, what we refer to as "clinical pearls"—practical suggestions and wisdom that others have found helpful but that have not been mentioned so far:

- If you are wondering if you need an evaluation for depression, get it. If you are depressed, you've taken the first step in getting better. If the clinician you see determines you need no further care, you have a baseline evaluation should your situation change in the future, you are known to a mental health professional, and any fee you have paid is worth it for all of this plus the reassurance.

• Speaking of fees, we all worry about the cost of mental health care. For clergy with insurance, whether through the church or through their spouses' policies, there is often a list of preferred providers whom third-party payers will reimburse at in-network rates. Do not fail to get treatment if you must pay out-of-network rates, as 50 to 60 percent reimbursement is still significant. Seminarians without insurance, or whose policies cover mental health care only poorly, should check with their student health centers, advisors, or deans. Many seminaries have clinicians they regularly refer to, often at reduced fees, and will help you troubleshoot whatever financial or other obstacles you might encounter in obtaining care. If anyone, regardless of benefits, lives reasonably close to a medical center, he or she should investigate if there are training programs in psychiatry, psychology, or pastoral care. Often the fees are quite low when clinicians in training, supervised in accredited programs, are the primary care providers.

• When antidepressant medications are recommended, it is often very reasonable to take generic preparations. However, some generics are not as effective for treatment as brand-name drugs or have other concerns associated with them. Please verify with the prescribing physician that he or she is comfortable with you taking a generic formulation.

• There are many complementary and alternative medicine (CAM) remedies touted for treatment of depression. These include herbals, vitamin, and mineral preparations and other various forms of "alternative remedies." Before beginning any CAM regimen, discuss it with your prescribing physician first. Also know that even though physicians' prescriptions may not be required to purchase these products, like any other medicine they can have side effects, toxicities, and interactions with other medications. Be sure to tell all physicians you see for any reason the names, doses, and reasons you are taking CAM products.

• I want to refer you back again to the section on suicide. If you are thinking of harming yourself, let someone know immediately and do not isolate yourself. If you are concerned that someone you know is thinking about harming himself or herself, get them help immediately. If you cannot go to the nearest emergency room or call 911 yourself, enlist someone to help you do so. The National Suicide Prevention Lifeline has a toll-free, 24-hour hotline: 1-800-273-TALK (1-800-273-8255).[33]

So What Happened to Sam Seminarian and Pamela Pastor?

Sam was referred for psychotherapy with a psychologist who was experienced with the issues of new seminarians. With the prayerful support of family, friends, his sponsoring denominational official, and his seminary advisor, Sam discerned that his gifts were better suited to lay ministry than ordained ministry with its required academic and "dressed up most of the time" requirements. That decision marked the

turning point in his depression, which also could have bene-
fited from antidepressant therapy on a short-term basis had he
chosen to avail himself of it. He returned to the camp ministry
he so loved, and appreciated the opportunities for growth and
continuing education that came his way in the form of management seminars, the occasional business or leadership class,
youth ministry workshops, and lay Bible classes. Employed by
his denomination, he was happy with the daily opportunities
he had to interact with clergy, youth, and parents of many,
many congregations through his camp ministry. He became
engaged to a young woman who was committed to lay ministry just as much as he was. About his depressive episode in
seminary, he said, "It was rough at the time, but I learned a
great deal about depression, and that should help me both
in my life later and in working with others. I'm really happy
with my camp administrator position, and people say it fits
me perfectly. Who knows, when I retire I might get a cabin
named after me!"

Pamela Pastor chose both individual psychotherapy and
antidepressant medication. She sings the praises of psychotherapy for not only helping her through the depression but
also helping her deal with her divorce many years ago and
allowing her to gain insights into how she sees herself and
interacts with others in her roles as single woman, mother,
and minister. She credits the antidepressant with improving
her mood, energy level, and sleep pattern. She has a renewed
interest in hobbies and friends and has lost twenty-five pounds
with a regular exercise program. Instead of seeing problems in
every corner and pew of her church, she is enthused about the
opportunities to energize her congregation's Christian education and community outreach programs.

Depression has long been one of the largest elephants in churches and in the lives of clergy, seminarians, and other religious professionals. Hopefully, the information in this chapter will help you acknowledge its existence and start to tame it!

Wild Elephants That Trample and Crush: A.K.A. "Dealing with Problematic Parishioners"

*As God's chosen ones, holy and beloved, clothe yourselves with
compassion, kindness, humility, meekness, and patience.
Bear with one another and, if anyone has a complaint against
another, forgive each other; just as the Lord has forgiven you,
so you also must forgive.
Above all, clothe yourselves in love, which binds everything together in
perfect harmony.
And let the peace of Christ rule in your hearts, to which indeed you
were called in the one body. And be thankful.*

The Elephant in the Church

Let the word of Christ dwell in you richly;
teach and admonish one another in all wisdom;
and with gratitude in your hearts
sing psalms, hymns, and spiritual songs to God.
And whatever you do, in word or deed, do everything in the name of
the Lord Jesus, giving thanks to God the Father through him.
Colossians 3:12-17 (NRSV)

I cannot tell you the number of times I have read or heard this passage and thought that if people could follow the guidance of these verses from Colossians, there would be much less agitation, anxiety, and fewer harsh words in this world. Let's face it—if we Christians could internalize and live out these words, there would be much less agitation, anxiety, and complaints in the church! Similarly, as a psychiatrist caring for patients and their families in the emergency department, on hospital medical floors, or for outpatient psychotherapy, I believe that doses of "compassion, kindness, humility, meekness, and patience" are helpful for almost everyone—especially clergy!

As we all know, though, some people are easier to like than others. Some folks require more compassion, kindness, and patience than their fair share, complain about everything, and seem unable or unwilling to forgive or be grateful. No matter what anyone says or does, things are too much, too little, too late, and never right. And they all seem to take up residence in our congregations, draining the compassion, kindness, and patience from the person they see as being paid to always demonstrate these qualities: the pastor.

Over the course of my work as a bivocational psychiatrist and clergywoman, I have led groups of medical professionals learning how to deal with difficult patients, supervised psychiatrists and other mental health clinicians learning to do psychotherapy, and worked with various groups of ministers and seminarians about how to work effectively with congregants and church leaders. While psychotherapy and the work of the pastor are two distinct career paths with distinguishable educational, training, and certification (ordination) requirements, these fields can and do overlap. In the daily jungle of parish life, this occurs when the minister is dealing with many kinds of people with diverse, often traumatic and troubled backgrounds. The purpose of this chapter is not to turn readers into diagnosticians or psychotherapists, but to acquaint clergy with some basic principles and observations about personality styles and behavior. This awareness can come in handy when dealing with the handful of rowdy elephants that reside in or circle around nearly every congregation.

Transference and Countertransference: What Every Pastor Should Know

Ms. Clara Cross,[1] a retired music teacher, had chaired the altar guild for decades when Rev. Joseph Cool arrived at First Church as the new associate pastor. A tall, single, outgoing, athletic man in his early thirties, Rev. Joe had a beautiful baritone singing voice that matched his wholesome, all-American good looks. After years of Rev. Boris "I'm-never-going-to-retire" Boring in the pulpit, the entire church was enchanted by the new preacher. Everyone, that is, except for Clara Cross. She criticized his wardrobe for being too stylish for a man of God, suspected every sermon or Bible lesson to be plagiarized from the Internet, regarded his popular solos as off-pitch or sung at the wrong tempo, and calculated that behind his every smile was an ulterior motive. Furthermore, if he had any appreciation for the hours of sacrifice the altar guild gave to make the sanctuary attractive on Sunday mornings, he wouldn't wrinkle the altar linens every time he set his Bible and hymnal down during worship! She e-mailed Rev. Joe several times a week with corrections, criticisms, and "helpful suggestions to assist during the probationary period of employment." She copied all e-mails and formal letters of complaint, complete with footnote references to Scripture, the church bylaws, and denominational policies and procedures, to Rev. Boris Boring, the chairs of the church elders, deacons, trustees, missionary societies, and all regional and national denominational officials.

After several months, Rev. Joe Cool found himself spending more time dealing with Clara Cross and the havoc she was stirring up than attending to his job responsibilities. He arranged a time to make a pastoral visit with Clara in her home. While this brief visit was cordial and relatively uneventful, he noticed an old black and white photograph of a young couple on the mantle. The young man in the picture looked uncannily similar to Rev. Joe. When he returned to the church office, he told Rev. Boring about the photo and asked what he knew about Clara's past. "Oh yes, a long time ago Clara was engaged to a young minister here in town. They were both musical and sang together around the county for different events. He left her for another woman a few days before their wedding, and she never got over it. Come to think of it, I guess you might remind her of him—tall, dark, handsome young preacher, and a good singer, too!"

Clara Cross's views, attitudes, and interactions with Rev. Joe Cool illustrate the concept of *transference*. Originating in the psychoanalytic literature, transference is a core concept in many different forms of psychotherapy. It refers to the fact that humans tend to experience and relate to new individuals based on past relationships and experiences they have had with others. We interpret what others say and do through the lens of what people in our past have said and done. Transference not only applies to the patient and psychotherapist relationship but is a part of all relationships and can play out daily in the parish, too. For instance, Clara's antagonistic attitudes and behaviors toward Rev. Joe really had nothing to do with him personally, but were instead the result of the unresolved emotions Clara harbored toward her fiancé from years ago. Rev. Joe's physical resemblance to her old beau, plus the fact that Joe was a minister who was a talented vocalist, was a set-up for Clara to unleash anger that had festered for years.

Closely related to transference in psychotherapy is the concept of *countertransference*, which is the transference or emotional reaction the therapist feels toward the patient. A well-trained therapist is able to recognize the feelings the patient evokes in her, then use them as tools to help her better understand the patient and the issues in therapy. For instance, if Rev. Joe is substituted for the psychotherapist as the authority figure, Rev. Joe might recognize he has ambivalent feelings, or countertransference, toward Clara Cross. On the one hand, she reminds him of his high school music teacher, who recognized his talent and got him out of a downward spiral of fights and after-school detentions by encouraging his talent and participation in choir and musical theater productions. On the other hand, Clara's constant nagging and criticisms remind him of his mother and grandmother, who still see him as a rebellious, delinquent teen instead of the upstanding man he has become. Applying the term *countertransference* to Rev. Joe might be resisted by some strict psychoanalysts who would say that only trained therapists can have countertransference—ministers simply have transference toward their parishioners. Regardless of which term is used, the point is that recognizing that others can elicit strong feelings from us based on our past relationships and experiences, which have nothing to do with the current situation, is very important. Understanding that relational truth can help us to match the most appropriate emotions and responses to the people and circumstances in the here and now, thereby keeping us out of trouble from time to time.[2]

Transference can be negative or positive.[3] Young women and young men who have been physically or sexually abused by their fathers or other men in authority may be reluctant to engage with a male pastor who shares similar qualities with their abusers, whether it be gender, voice quality, age, hair color, or the presence of a beard. It does not mean that the majority of abuse victims cannot form a healthy minister/church member relationship, just that the religious professional may need to be more patient and relate to the individual in a different way than he or she otherwise might. The example of Clara Cross's transference to Rev. Joe Cool illustrates negative transference. On the other hand, a middle-aged, graying male pastor may remind a thirty-something-year-old father of a favorite uncle or sports coach, and that high regard transferred to the pastor might be instrumental in drawing the father into congregational life. This is an example of positive transference. We should be alert to the fact that pastors are at risk for being over-valued or idolized, reflecting a parishioner's perceptions of or attributions toward God. However, we should also be aware that pastors are vulnerable to being devalued, scorned, or even hated if identified too closely with a deity blamed for tragedies, losses, or catastrophes.[4] Rev. Joe Cool was insightful enough to know that he did not have the psychotherapeutic skills and training to address the multiple layers of Clara Cross's transference toward him. Recognition of that transference helped him to be more patient with Clara, not to take her criticisms personally, and to better appreciate her strengths, talents, and contributions she made every week to the life of the church.

Defense Mechanisms

The term "herd of elephants" is actually not a bad way to describe defense mechanisms, which can emerge like a "herd instinct" in the presence of change, challenge, pain, or threat. Humans tend to react in predictable ways to strong emotions and to new or stressful situations. *Defense mechanisms* are ways of thinking and dealing with the world, and they serve to prevent the experiencing of uncomfortable, painful feelings and conflicts. They are styles of reacting to perceived real or potential problems that are long-standing. Defense mechanisms are usually so automatic that we do not even realize we are using them unless they are pointed out to us, most commonly by a therapist or counselor. The knowledge that both churchgoers and pastors often respond to stressors in characteristic ways can be helpful for tipping us off when something in an interaction has gone awry. This knowledge equips us in predicting how certain individuals will think and act in particularly difficult situations, and in demonstrating patience through initial reactions until the problem or concern at hand can be addressed in a mature, productive fashion.[5]

Defense mechanisms can be considered to reside on a continuum from *primitive* to *mature*. The more mature or adaptive defense mechanisms are also called *coping mechanisms*. Let's review some common defense and coping mechanisms, from the most primitive to the most adaptive, and how we might encounter them in the church.

- **Repression:** Pushing painful or unacceptable desires and impulses out of awareness. Example: A Sunday school teacher in an unhappy marriage experiences a fleeting moment of attraction to another woman's husband. However, such a feeling of attraction is so antithetical to her religious and moral beliefs and behaviors that she immediately puts it out of her mind and would be hard-pressed to remember she ever felt a forbidden attraction in the first place.

- **Denial:** Exhibiting the inability or refusal to acknowledge a painful truth or reality, whether about oneself or others. Example: The same Sunday school teacher, if confronted by another person about the possibility of being attracted to anyone other than her spouse, would be unable to acknowledge this would ever happen to her.

- **Splitting:** Experiencing other people and situations as either all good or all bad, unable to tolerate that an idealized individual is not perfect. Example: One Sunday morning, the senior pastor forgot to mention the birth of a prominent couple's first grandchild during the morning announcements. The associate pastor noticed the omission and worked a thanksgiving for the birth into her benediction. From that time on, the senior pastor could do nothing right, and the associate became a shining star. The devaluation of the senior and idealization of the junior clergyperson spread to others in the congregation due to the influence of this particular couple, and the splitting became detrimental to the life of the congregation.

- **Reaction formation:** Changing from one unacceptable or unwanted thought or action to an opposite thought or action to avoid emotional discomfort or pain. Example: The fear of being late to worship, finding all the back pews filled, and having to walk in shame to the front of the sanctuary prompts a man to arrive ten minutes before the organist starts the prelude every Sunday morning.

- **Displacement:** Redirecting strong feelings or thoughts onto someone or something else. Example: A group of women cannot believe their congregation is aging and losing membership to the extent that the church board would vote to turn the church nursery into a storage room. Instead, they blame the new pastor for the sequence of events leading to the demise of the nursery room space, claiming her poor preaching and lack of understanding of the congregation's history in that community is driving the church to die and close its doors.

- **Regression:** Returning to thoughts and behaviors of a less mature or younger developmental or adaptation level to avoid conflict. Example: A prominent businessman in the congregation has chaired the property and grounds committee for years. Now the businessman is past retirement and in the early stages of cognitive slowing, and his adult son has new and creative ideas for building and grounds use that are also financially astute. Instead of speaking confidently about his ideas at committee meetings, the younger man retreats, apologizes, says, "Yes, sir," and even becomes tearful occasionally when his aging father tells him to sit down and shut up because "we've never done it that way before." The son finds standing up to his father so painful that he backs away from conflict, from "embarrassing" his father, or from outshining the older man, by reacting in a very regressed, even inappropriately immature manner.

- **Conversion:** Expressing forbidden or unacceptable thoughts or wishes via physical, bodily symptoms. Example: A beloved matriarch in the parish family was facing financial difficulties and became unable to maintain the large house she had shared with her now-deceased husband. The house held many fond memories, including many Sunday School class parties and holiday celebrations. Whenever family and friends gently but firmly confronted her about the need to make decisions about the house, she developed severe headaches and abdominal pain with no diagnosable medical cause, requiring hospitalizations and resulting in significant expressions of concern from clergy and church members.

- **Intellectualization:** Dealing with emotionally charged or painful feelings by focusing exclusively on detailed facts and cognitive explanations. Example: A science teacher in the congregation was diagnosed with an extremely aggressive, invasive form of cancer. He dealt with the diagnosis by researching and learning everything he could about the illness, to the extreme of looking up new treatments on his laptop even as he was sent home from the hospital with hospice care. While his coping style enabled him to work with his medical team and tend to treatment details, it also deprived him and his loved ones of precious time to share important words and feelings until just minutes before his death.

- **Sublimation:** Using a mature defense or coping mechanism that channels hurt, disappointment, and unacceptable thoughts and feelings into adaptive, productive, socially acceptable outlets. Example: A very responsible, faithful member of the parish was nominated for a position on the vestry, or church board. He received the fewest number of votes of the several candidates running for the three open positions. Though disappointed that he was not elected, he looked for other ways to be helpful. The local homeless shelter and the van ministry to take elderly members to worship services became the grateful recipients of his time and service after the parish election.[6]

While psychoanalysts and psychotherapy experts include several other defense or coping mechanisms on their complete lists, most pastors will recognize the nine described above as relatively common coping styles in congregants and church staff as well.

Personality Traits and Disorders

Thanks to popular psychology and afternoon talk shows, the term *personality disorder* is familiar to many, if not most, ministers. Though psychiatrists and psychotherapists adhere to strict diagnostic criteria when speaking of personality disorders, in the common vernacular it has come to have many varied, nontechnical, even pejorative meanings. Many of my consultations with pastors and congregations have included questions relating to personality traits versus more disturbing and, presumably entrenched, personality disorders.

Personality traits are distinguishing qualities or characteristics that help make us who we are as individuals. They are the result of many complex interactions and combinations of developmental, experiential, psychological, cultural, and genetic or inherited factors. They are also informed by our temperaments, which in turn have been shown to be strongly influenced by heredity. Traits begin to take shape in childhood, with some becoming established early on in life and others being shaped continually over adolescence and young adulthood. Some traits are viewed as primarily helpful and adaptive, others as always problematic, and still others as relatively neutral depending upon the situation in which they are displayed. Experts in personality theory tend to agree that achieving a stable, positive sense of self and the ability to form mutually gratifying and long-lasting relationships are two key signs of healthy personality development.[7]

Personality disorders occur when personality traits exist in patterns that are inflexible, maladaptive, distressing to the individual and others around him or her, and cause significant difficulties or impairment in personal, occupational, and other spheres of life.[8] *The Diagnostic and Statistical Manual of Mental Disorders*, Fourth Edition, Text Revision, lists ten specific personality disorders, including paranoid, schizoid, schizotypal, antisocial, borderline, histrionic, narcissistic, avoidant, dependent, and obsessive-compulsive.[9] Studies estimate that more than 50 percent of patients seen in clinical settings have personality disorders, making these maladies the most common diagnosis seen by mental health professionals.[10] At least 12 percent of the general population, or those not receiving any mental health care, are estimated to have personality disorders.[11] Once again, the purpose of this section is not a crash course in personality pathology. However, given the pervasiveness of personality disorders in society at large, it behooves ministers to have some familiarity with mental health issues.

The unhealthy patterns of understanding others and behaving in the world that are inherent to personality disorders especially affect an individual's ability to keep a steady mood, control impulses, and relate well and reliably to others. These issues are evident by at least late adolescence and young adulthood and endure throughout the life span, though to varying degrees as one ages. These difficulties are seen at home with family, in dating and romantic relationships, in marriages, and at work with coworkers and bosses. They are also seen in recreational, or "play," contexts. Personality-disordered individuals are also characterized by inflexibility of emotional and behavioral responses. The universality of relationship and behavior issues extends to the church, where relationships are not only with other humans, but also with the Divine, and where problematic behaviors can interfere with or complicate the mission and work of congregations.

While the distinction between personality *traits* and personality *disorders* is important academically and in clinical settings, distinguishing between the two categories in the "real world" is often challenging. All of us have certain traits and ways of responding to stress that can be upsetting, inappropriate, and counter-productive when we are in the midst of crises small or large. When working with parishioners, sometimes it can be difficult to figure out if a particular behavior is the person's usual way of operating or a one-time reaction that results in a poor way of handling a situation. However, the practical implications of longer-term personality problems, whether disorders or extreme traits, are significant. These individuals are at greater risk than are those with stable, predictable moods and behavior patterns for unfulfilling marriages, separation, divorce, and child custody disputes. They experience more job instability, unemployment, homelessness, substance abuse, accidents, police contacts, and emergency department care and medical hospitalizations. They can be involved with violence and have higher rates of self-injurious behaviors and completed suicides than do those without personality issues.[12] It should be obvious that clergy frequently are involved in these scenarios, whether called by the individual, a spouse, or other family members. Often, clergy must try to assist and support all affected in between crisis events.

One particular personality disorder or set of traits that can be especially frustrating for clergy are *borderline personality disorders* or *borderline traits*. Individuals with borderline tendencies have difficulty with emotional attachments and separations, see people and situations as "all good" or "all bad" (*splitting*), and are subject to rages and severe irritability and moodiness. They have an unstable self-image or sense of self and chronic feelings of emptiness. They are impulsive and therefore susceptible to substance abuse, disordered eating, sexual acting out, reckless driving, spending money, and other indiscretions. They are prone to self-injurious behaviors and suicide attempts.[13] The sincere caretaking proclivities of pastors make us a nice foil to their never-ending neediness. The enduring, long-lasting nature of the church and its message of the unconditional love of God offers the promise of acceptance and tranquility that is especially consoling for those suffering from borderline tendencies.

So, What's a Pastor to Do?

To avoid being trampled and trampling on others unintentionally, ministers in the twenty-first century must be aware of the elephants of transference, primitive defense mechanisms, and maladaptive personality styles. This does not mean we ignore or water down the mandates of scripture to minister to the broken-hearted, the mentally ill, and those in prison or on parole or probation. Instead, awareness of potential pitfalls, being alert to boundary issues, and knowing when to set limits and ask for help are qualities of a mature pastor. Here are some suggestions to consider:

1. **Be aware of appropriate boundaries.** Even if the pastor is perfectly well behaved and all intentions are pure, it is important to avoid behaviors that might be misunderstood or misinterpreted by others—especially parishioners dealing with

some of the personality, intimacy, and dependency issues mentioned earlier. In mental health, a boundary is considered to be the edge of appropriate behavior. Thoughtful boundaries can establish safe and predictable atmospheres in which ministry can thrive. As I tell both seminarians and medical trainees, maintaining good professional boundaries is more than just abstaining from sexual behaviors with those for whom they care. Clergy should avoid meeting alone in the church office with vulnerable parishioners, especially after hours. Care should be taken when having church members in one's home, not just in terms of being alone, but also remembering that even items such as personal photographs and mementos may reveal information about the pastor that he or she might not choose to disclose otherwise. Clearly, the type of church and the size and location of the community in which one is living influence what boundaries can be implemented. For instance, in a rural community, the only plumber to deal with a bathroom plumbing emergency or the only veterinarian to euthanize a beloved, aged family pet might be a church member. However, in larger communities, it is easier to keep certain boundaries. It could be considered a boundary violation to have a parishioner with borderline traits, whom you have visited in the hospital on multiple occasions after suicide attempts, drop off your dry cleaning at the church after hours, even if the company she works for has the best prices and honors coupons. For a few of our parishioners, even an innocent, brief touch of the hand on the shoulder by the pastor can be misunderstood. And while some self-disclosure in sermons can be effective in getting a point across, some preachers are too honest and descriptive when it comes to their own past sins and personal lives, when blander generalizations would get the job done well enough. Does this mean pastors should not share and emote with church members and those to whom they minister? Not at all—just be aware of what unintended meanings may be received by particular individuals based on their personality styles and personal circumstances.[14]

2. **Keep as much of your schedule as possible transparent, even when dealing with sensitive people and material.** Keep your schedule recorded in such a way that, if called upon to do so later, you can account for your time and location. Whether done on paper or a computer calendar, you can note initials and locations of meetings in such a way that confidentiality of the content of your pastoral work is not compromised and you can minimize any doubts about your professionalism. As much as you can, make sure another person on the church staff knows where you are and, in general terms at least, what you are doing when you are working.

3. **Remember that in nearly all jurisdictions, clergy are mandated reporters of abuse and neglect, especially of minors.** Reporting suspected abuse

and neglect is never something to be taken light-
ly. Many, if not most, denominations have man-
datory education and reporting requirements,
emphasizing that clergy confidentiality does not
apply to situations in which others are either being hurt or at risk of being hurt. Pastors should
familiarize themselves with the applicable laws in
the states in which they serve, as well as denominational resources regarding this issue of reporting abuse and neglect within their congregations.
Obtaining structure and care for both the abuser
and abused can be great gifts to all involved, even
if it is not evident at the time.

4. **Take seriously all threats to commit suicide or
   homicide, or to harm self or others.** When concerned about the safety of a parishioner and others whom the person might be at risk of harming,
   the pastor should ask directly and simply, "Are
   you thinking about harming or killing yourself or
   anyone else?" then obtain immediate assistance if
   answered affirmatively. Calling a family member
   to come assist and making sure the individual is
   not alone until a family member arrives can be
   appropriate if one is sure the family member will
   take the individual for psychiatric assessment immediately. However, calling 911 for assistance in
   taking the parishioner to an emergency room is
   always a good idea, and the timely call by a clergyperson in such situations can be lifesaving. Occasionally, one can convince parishioners in crisis
   to seek immediate help on their own volition,
   but helping them access emergency services is

considered a safer, more reliable way to guarantee an emergency assessment and appropriate timely treatment.

5. **Refer to mental health clinicians, even when an individual is not actively harmful to self or others.** Use caution and try to avoid being both parish priest *and* psychotherapist at the same time, even if you have appropriate training in both areas. Maintain a list of community resources, such as male and female therapists, psychologists, psychiatrists, pastoral counselors, rape crisis centers, emergency rooms, medical clinics, and homeless shelters, and keep them in your wallet, purse, or smart phone. Many denominations and states have rules and regulations about how many counseling or individual sessions congregational ministers can have with someone before he or she must be referred to an outside mental health professional—make sure you know what policies apply to you and your ministry settings.

6. **Find a supervisory group, such as a group composed of other parish clergy discussing difficult pastoral relationships with a mental health clinician, for the purpose of supervision and feedback regarding challenging relationships and situations within the congregational setting.** There can be many benefits to this. First, delicate situations can be recognized and dealt with earlier than they might be otherwise. Second, this is a great vehicle for keeping up with new information, getting "second opinions," and growing as a

clergyperson. Also, pastoral work can be isolating, and feeling isolated can lead to discouragement and contribute to clergy burnout. Many clergy I know value this type of group tremendously. If time and finances permit, individual supervision with a psychologist or psychiatrist on these issues can also be quite helpful.

7. **Get into your own personal psychotherapy.** To deal as effectively as possible with the transferences, defenses, and personalities we handle day after day in congregational ministry, we can all benefit from working with someone well trained, neutral, and outside the parish. The more we know about ourselves and understand our own past experiences, preferred coping styles and defenses, and adaptive (and occasionally maladaptive and imperfect!) personality traits, the better we can serve our churches *and* maintain and grow in our spiritual, emotional, and professional lives. If your insurance reimburses too poorly or you have no insurance at all to cover personal psychotherapy, contact pastoral care programs near you, as well as psychiatry, psychology, and other psychotherapy training programs. Often, these organizations are professional homes for well-qualified clinicians and have sliding fee scales available.

It is impossible to name all the different kinds of elephants that can step on the toes of pastors as they minister to God's children who have been hurt in the past, are hurting now, and are behaving in ways that continue to hurt themselves and others. The reality is that many do not have good resiliency or coping skills and will try to test all your gifts and graces for pastoral ministry. Hopefully, this chapter has been helpful by reminding us of the different kinds of personality traits and behavioral patterns many church members exhibit. While we should be aware of these issues, we should not become too paranoid or discouraged that we cannot continue to minister in very serious situations. For me, the good news is that the church has served as the greatest community mental health center since its inception twenty centuries ago. The even greater news is that the church is still here now and welcoming to all regardless of our quirks, foibles, and pathologies.

Prayer for the Unity of the Church

O God the Father of our Lord Jesus Christ, our only Savior, the Prince of Peace:

Give us grace seriously to lay to heart the great dangers we are in by our unhappy divisions;

take away all hatred and prejudice, and whatever else may hinder us from godly union and concord;

that, as there is but one Body and one Spirit, one hope of our calling,

one Lord, one Faith, one Baptism, one God and Father of us all,

so we may be all of one heart and of one soul, united in one holy bond of truth and peace, of faith and charity,

and may with one mind and one mouth glorify thee;

through Jesus Christ our Lord. Amen.

The Book of Common Prayer *(1979), p. 818*

Chapter Six

And the Elephant in the Room Is . . . the Preacher!

Beloved, I pray that all may go well with you, and that you may be in good health, just as it is well with your soul.
3 John 1:2 (NRSV)

One of my first positions after finishing my medical training was with a clergy health service at a large medical center. One of its functions was to connect ministers, seminarians, and other religious professionals with appropriate medical services when they became ill and regular health care and preventive services to keep them well. I learned a great deal about clergy health and wellness during those years. I also learned from their experiences of illness, and in a few instances, the gift of accompanying them through the valley of the shadow of death.

Pastors are trained to listen and minister to the needs of others. Their job is to keep the church running on the inside while leading and coaching its missionary and prophetic presence in the community and world on the outside. This takes immeasurable time, energy, and spiritual and emotional commitment. It relies heavily on one's intellect and social skills. Long and unpredictable work days are part of the pastor's package. We grab food on the go and spend countless hours sitting in the car, in hospital waiting rooms, on parishioners' sofas, in staff and church committee meetings, and—if we can find the time—at the desk and computer preparing sermons and managing all those e-mails and voicemails and text messages. One cannot help but understand why care of the physical body often comes in a distant last in the race for the preacher's time and commitment. For reasons that are all unselfish, understandable, and true, the best intentions for good self-care of even the most athletic and disciplined clergyperson can be ambushed repeatedly.

As we travel through this chapter, please remember that in most respects, when it comes to health and wellness practices, clergy are no different from many, if not most, Americans. The last several years have seen increased attention by our society to the role of lifestyle and behaviors, especially as they influence our health. An awareness of some very basic facts in this area may benefit pastors regarding their own well-being *and* better equip them to understand and minister to their congregants with medical concerns.

As we continue, remember that the sole purpose of this chapter is to share general information about a few general health topics, thereby raising awareness about these and clergy self-care in its intended audience. Readers concerned that they or someone else they know or care about might have health concerns should consult their own physicians or other qualified clinicians for appropriate assessment, diagnosis, and treatment of all medical concerns.

"The Facts, Ma'am, Nothing but the Facts"

Such has been the mantra of many a TV crime-show detective over the years. When it comes to health and lifestyle, we've all noticed that information can shift and some recommendations flip-flop. For instance, as I was growing up, eggs for breakfast were great sources of protein to start the day, and you could never go wrong drinking milk regularly for calcium and vitamin D (whole was the only kind I remember seeing in our small town grocery as a child). Now we are bombarded with commercials advising us to limit eggs to reduce our cholesterol and pour skim milk on our whole grain fiber cereals to avoid the fat content of whole milk and keep our bowels regular. It's hard to keep straight from day to day whether a glass of wine a day increases longevity, or if it should be totally shunned. The same for caffeine and chocolate—should I or should I not partake, and if so, one cup or two, dark chocolate or white?

In other words, "It's complicated." The relationships between health attitudes and behaviors—what we do and have influence over—and risk factors for disease are complex. A *risk factor* is a condition that can make us more vulnerable to an illness or accident. For instance, not wearing seat belts increases the chances of severe injuries for passengers in automobile accidents. Some risk factors can be changed or modified, while others cannot. For instance, risk factors for heart disease include age, family history, gender, high blood pressure, smoking, obesity, sedentary lifestyle, and diabetes. We cannot change our age, sex, and family health histories, but we often can modify or change our activity level and nutrition, and cut down on or stop smoking.[1]

In recent years, heart disease, cancer (all forms), stroke, chronic lung disease, and diabetes have been ranked in the top ten leading causes of death in adults by numerous government and health agencies.[2] An estimated 100 million adults in the United States are overweight or obese, and being overweight increases the possibility of gallbladder disease, sleep problems, joint damage, and breast, colon, uterine, and gall bladder cancers.[3] Because obesity is a well-known and accepted risk factor for these and other conditions, and because many clergy struggle with being overweight and are as susceptible to these diseases as everyone else, let's consider this elephant right now.

The Overweight Elephant and Its Care

Many years ago, I was having lunch in a seminary cafeteria with a clergy colleague and mentor as part of an event attended by many experienced ministers. An open buffet had been set up in the center of the large, rectangular dining room to accommodate the larger than usual lunch crowd of regular students and seminary personnel, plus the workshop attendees. From our table, my friend and I had a good view of the students and ministers going through the line and filling their plates with food. We were struck by (as were others sitting near us), and could not avoid, the observation of several significantly overweight students and ministers returning to the buffet stations for second, third, even fourth ample helpings of fried foods and desserts. While the physician part of me had visions of clogged coronary arteries (blood vessels in the heart) and fatty livers flash before my eyes, my friend was just as troubled by what we witnessed, if not more so. He had served as a missionary in an area of the world where hunger predominates, parents struggle to feed their families, and opportunities for education are limited, a stark contrast to the abundance of opportunities and resources, including healthy meals, common in settings of American theological education.

Certainly, this buffet scene is not unique to seminaries, clergy gatherings, or any other church setting. This was at least a decade ago, when the medical community and lay media were first starting to hint that being overweight, physically inactive, and eating poorly were going to be major public health issues in the twenty-first century. My friend and I wondered about possible theological and pastoral aspects of these issues and possible prophetic and pastoral roles the church might have in the years to come. Several conversations ensued about care of our bodies as part of our stewardship of God's gifts, and how churches could model good stewardship and care of God's gift of embodiment by raising awareness of health matters and adopting healthier practices in the regular life of the congregation. Because this had not been written about or broached very much in churches at that time, we wrote a brief op-ed piece for a denominational news publication. We suggested that eating behaviors and caring for one's body indeed can be considered through the lens of stewardship and that churches might consider small steps toward fostering a healthy congregation, such as substituting healthier foods for frosted donuts at Sunday morning coffee hours.

While we received many comments agreeing with the necessity of addressing preventive health in faith communities and discussing how to ease into conversations about healthy lifestyles in venues already common in congregational life, we were surprised a few months later to read a letter taking issue with the very general statement that lifestyle was one of the most significant contributors to the increased numbers of overweight individuals and criticizing us as promoting a stigma of obese people from the pulpit. The writer of the letter missed the fact that by including this issue as one of many elements of earthly life that affect our physical, emotional, and spiritual health—and consequently our ability to serve God and others—the church can model healthier living both inside and outside its walls. Certainly, the explosion of parish nursing programs, new clinics, and health care by many churches as part of their outreach programs and the ever-growing literature that has emerged in the last several years has supported and expanded upon the reflections we wrote about in our brief commentary a decade ago.

Ministers are not unlike others in many walks of life who, as a group, have watched the numbers on the scales rise, thus increasing risk factors for a number of serious medical conditions and predisposing them to fatigue and less stamina personally and professionally. In particular, clergy work long hours, commonly attend meetings over lunch or refreshments, and feel awkward declining a piece of homemade chocolate cake when they go for a home visit with a new family in their congregation. As the years go by, responsibilities that can only be done while seated seem to increase, and it becomes more and more difficult to work in exercise. And, oh, all those pitch-in dinners! So what's a preacher to do?

Tending to the Cornerstones of Eating Right and Keeping Fit

As with most subjects these days, it helps to know the language. **Body Mass Index (BMI)** is now agreed to be a more accurate indicator of obesity than the traditional unit of pounds. You can ask your physician or nurse to help you, or you can use one of several online calculators (such as the one available in the patient education resources section of the American College of Physicians website, www.acponline.org) to help you determine your BMI. A BMI less than 18.5 is considered to be underweight for both men and women, a BMI between 18.5 and 25.0 is within normal limits, a BMI of 25.0 and 29.9 is overweight, and a BMI of 30.0 or greater is considered to be obese. This highest BMI category is roughly equivalent to at least 20 percent more than the maximum healthy weight for a person's height.[4] Knowing your starting point helps you work with your physician to determine the safest nutrition and fitness strategies with the greatest likelihood of success for you.

My observation is that the nature of clergy schedules and types of eating occasions—pitch-in dinners and lots of meetings with refreshments consisting of coffee, soft drinks, and pastries—predispose one to a high-carbohydrate, high-fat diet. Even as pastors successfully decrease their caloric intake, it can be difficult to eat a balanced diet with the proper nutrients, vitamins, and minerals to foster optimal health and well-being. In addition to working with your physician, nutritionist, or other professional recommended by your doctor, I recommend the website ChooseMyPlate.gov (www.choosemyplate.gov). Developed and maintained by the United States Department of Agriculture, it has much information for all ages, male and female, about nutritional requirements, the different food groups, sample recipes, and planning meals on a budget. ChooseMyPlate.gov is a great source for information on diet, physical activity, and other educational materials.

Most clergy are familiar with the benefits of exercise. We hear and read about these quite a bit now, whether in the news media or in advertisements for sports drinks, prescription medications, or athletic gear. In addition to helping to control our weight, exercise strengthens muscles, helps our sleep, reduces stress and anxiety, keeps our bones healthy and strong, and maintains our strength and flexibility. Mild to moderate exercise decreases the risk of diabetes and some cancers, lowers cholesterol, helps control blood pressure, and lowers the risk of heart disease. *Cardiovascular (aerobic) exercise* burns calories, which is important for weight loss, builds endurance, and works your heart and lungs to improve the body's ability to use oxygen efficiently. Walking, running, swimming, bicycling, and skiing are examples of cardiovascular exercise. *Strength training* exerts force on muscles and bones to make them stronger. Building muscle improves muscle tone, helping the body burn calories even better. Sit-ups, push-ups, leg lifts, and weight training are common forms of strength training.[5]

While there are some fine athletes in our ranks, I'm sure that many of us are "pew warmers" and likely will be starting from scratch in any fitness endeavor after a long period of relative inactivity. Before starting an exercise program, or if you think you might be "discerning a call" to increase your physical activity, speak with your primary care physician to obtain his or her blessing and make sure there are no concerns or stipulations on exercise for you that you may not know. Start out very slowly, under supervision of either the physician or a reputable trainer. Taking stairs instead of elevators, parking a bit farther away from the doors of the building under well-lit safe conditions, taking a 5- or 10-minute walk during lunch time, or increasing the pace of regular housework or gardening chores can be painless first efforts at increasing energy expenditures and improving one's condition. Several health organizations publish guidelines for beginning exercise slowly and increasing gradually in such a way as to minimize self-injury. Your physician should be able to recommend the program or guidelines best suited to your needs. You will be more likely to continue if you select an activity you enjoy, find a consistent time of the day, and find a partner or "kindred spirit" with whom you enjoy spending some time and who enjoys similar workouts or activities. Many people find that varying the routine and forms of exercise keeps the endeavor fresh.

The National Institutes of Health (NIH) published some weight control tips in a recent newsletter that clergy may find helpful:

- **Use nutrition labels.** Don't guess how many calories you're eating.

- **Watch your portions.** Value-size servings aren't a bargain if you're eating too much.

- **Cut the sugar.** Don't let sugary soda or other sweets crowd out health.

- **Don't eat out of habit.** Mindless eating at work or in front of the TV can pack on pounds.

- **Think about the whole meal,** not just the main course.

- **Use smaller dishes and containers.** Larger ones encourage you to eat more.

- **Keep reminders of how much you're eating.** Wrappers, empty containers, and bones nearby remind you of how much you've eaten.

- **Get enough sleep.** Less sleep is linked to higher rates of obesity.

- **Get active.** Look for opportunities to add physical activity to your daily routine.

- **Do it together.** Family, friends, and coworkers can all help each other make healthy changes to their lives.[6]

The purpose of naming the obesity elephant among us is not to be judgmental, foster stigma, or be callous to the numerous challenges we face daily as we care for others and juggle competing responsibilities in our personal and professional lives. One's physical habitus is the result of many factors, some of which we have little control over, such as genetics and family history. However, most clergy accept that minimizing alcohol consumption is advisable if one is at risk for substance dependence, and that non-smokers display decreased vulnerabilities to a myriad of other health problems. Tending to one's diet and activity level are widely accepted methods in health care today to lower risk factors for illnesses aggravated or worsened by excessive weight. As the plethora of information in the last decade has illustrated, the elephants of overweight and inactivity do not discriminate on the basis of gender, age, ethnicity, socioeconomic class, marital status, or educational level. Yes, these elephants have expanded their reach in recent years, and it is fitting to be aware not only of their affinities for pews and pulpits, but of reasonable, attainable management strategies.

Keep Those Health Care Appointments, Even Though You Think You're Fine!

Reverend John Doe[7] noticed a small, raised, circular white patch on the side of his tongue in the back of his mouth when he was brushing his teeth one summer day. It wasn't painful, so he dismissed it as something that would go away and did not pay any attention to its very gradual growth over subsequent weeks. A pastoral emergency forced him to cancel a dental appointment shortly thereafter. Several weeks later, his wife encouraged him to see his physician when she noticed several enlarged lymph nodes below his ear and on the side of his neck. John responded that he had not had any fevers and he felt fine, so he did not see a reason to try to fit an appointment into his busy schedule. He never noticed that the white patch had grown into a lump on his tongue until some tissue sloughed off during the first week of Advent, causing bleeding and pain. Of course, Advent and Christmas were very busy at church, so Rev. Doe made an appointment with his physician when his schedule slowed down after Epiphany. The oral lesion and enlarged lymph nodes proved to be a form of head and neck cancer. Both Rev. Doe and his physician wondered if the malignancy might have been diagnosed earlier if he had kept his original dental appointment the previous fall or scheduled a doctor's appointment when Mrs. Doe noticed his prominent lymph nodes.

***

The Rev. Lettie Late-Bloomer, a forty-five-year-old divorced, second-career pastor in a rural community, supplemented her part-time church position with substitute teaching. She had always been healthy and never needed health insurance in the past, so she had not been worried when at age forty she declined insurance through her denominational plan until "a few years later, when I'm on a solid financial footing and can afford it better." In the meantime, she experienced a couple of years of lengthy menstrual periods with heavy bleeding. She would have gone to a doctor about the blood loss sooner, but she was busy. She didn't want to have to pay the full cost of the visit out-of-pocket; there was no family history of cancer, and she assumed she simply was having "a rough menopause." One Sunday morning when she did not show up to lead worship, the church pianist found her passed out on the floor of her home. Thankfully, the Rev. Late-Bloomer did not have cancer, but had fainted due to the cumulative tolls of blood loss and anemia. She gradually returned to her previous state of good health after appropriate diagnosis and treatment.

***

Even if ministers and seminarians are trim, exercise, and eat well, we must pay attention to recommendations for routine medical care and guidelines for regular health screenings. It is your health care provider's responsibility to guide you in this process and to make sure your care plan is developed with your specific concerns, family history, risk, and resiliency factors in mind. Having met and cared for many religious professionals who postponed or neglected preventive care—even if the reasons why initially made sense and seemed noble—I feel obligated to sing the praises, merits, and benefits of health maintenance visits and adherence to screening guidelines whenever possible.

The U.S. Preventive Services Task Force (USPSTF) publishes and regularly updates recommendations for preventive services in *The Guide to Clinical Preventive Services*.[8] These recommendations are based on the strictest available medical evidence regarding prevention strategies shown effective in improving patient outcomes. The report covers both sexes and all age groups, ethnicities, and special patient populations, such as pregnant women. Conditions addressed include cancers, diabetes, cardiovascular diseases, sexually transmitted diseases, osteoporosis in older women, smoking, and other substance abuse—just to name a few. Screening recommendations take into account risk factors and previous screening results, and vary even within the same disease category based on these and other considerations. In many instances, the USPSTF recommendations have been adopted or endorsed by other medical organizations, such as the American Academy of Family Practice, the American Urological Association, and the American College of Preventive Medicine.[9] Nearly all physicians who care for clergy will be members of these guilds, be trained in programs teaching the importance of authoritative guidelines such as these, and/or have access to up-to-date screening recommendations.

Specific and detailed information about screening measures, ages at which screening should be implemented, and time intervals for repeat screening are beyond the purview of this chapter, nor are these the goals here. What is important is that ministers of all ages and in all states of health partner with their physicians and other health care providers to determine appropriate preventive health care based on personal and family risk factors and relative risk/benefit ratios of screening measures.

****

Sleep

I will both lie down and sleep in peace; for you alone,
O LORD, make me lie down in safety.
Psalm 4:8 (NRSV)

For many of us, lying down and enjoying peaceful, restorative sleep just does not happen every night, if at all. Sleep is undoubtedly an overlooked factor in the health and well-being of clergy. As we have mentioned, sleep can be affected by and symptomatic of depression, anxiety, and numerous medical illnesses. Sleep disturbances occurring several nights a month are reported by as much as 30 percent of the general population. Primary sleep disorders impair daytime functioning and occupational performance, contribute to cardiovascular disease, endocrine problems, and various pain issues, and are risk factors for motor vehicle accidents. Individuals with sleep issues may use excessive amounts of alcohol, prescription medications, and over-the-counter sleep preparations to get to sleep, then turn around and drink large volumes of coffee and use stimulants to stay awake during the day.[10]

Sleep medicine is a new but rapidly growing specialty, and a number of different sleep disorders have been categorized. You may have heard the terms *dyssomnia, primary insomnia, hypersomnia, narcolepsy,* and *circadian rhythm sleep disorder* discussed on news shows or in commercials for medications to treat these disorders.[11]

Of the formal sleep disorders, in my practice I have seen more clergy struggling with obstructive sleep disorder than with any other single, discrete sleep diagnosis. In sleep apnea, the upper airway intermittently becomes occluded or obstructed during the course of sleep.

When these obstructions limit the free passage of air from the nose, throat, and neck structures to the lungs, blood oxygen levels drop, and the individual experiences very brief periods of arousals. Bed partners report loud snoring and gasping during sleep, in addition to periods of ten seconds or longer when the affected individual does not breathe at all despite efforts to do so. Sleep apnea can cause or aggravate daytime fatigue, high blood pressure, heart disease, and trouble with memory, concentration, and other cognitive processes.

My clinical observation and experience of an increase in the prevalence of sleep apnea is consistent with what many physicians are seeing across the country in recent years coincidental with the rapid increase in obesity and physical inactivity. Increased weight, especially in the neck and chest, adds to the resistance the lungs, diaphragm, and chest wall must overcome to permit a deep breath. It is quite common that clergy report significantly improved sleep, sharpness, and clarity of thought as they address health issues predisposing them to obstructive sleep apnea.[12]

Other sleep concerns I hear about from clergy do not constitute specific disorders, but instead are lifestyle and behavioral factors that in turn affect sleep quality. Irregular schedules, chronic stress, poor diets, and inadequate exercise contribute to suboptimal sleep. In general, most of us are over-scheduled, and we have not been conditioned to thinking of sleep as a necessary physiological process that needs to be respected and nurtured just as we care for other aspects of our body. The term *sleep hygiene* refers to habits and behaviors around our sleeping, whether at night or during the day. Physicians, psychologists, and other professionals who treat sleep disorders regularly instruct individuals with sleep problems to incorporate these recommendations into their lives as a non-pharmacological treatment or in combination with medicine if drug treatment is required. Key elements of good sleep hygiene include the following:

- Have consistent bedtimes and wake up at the same time every day, regardless of when you fell asleep.

- Avoid caffeine or nicotine for a minimum of six hours before bedtime.

- Drink alcohol only minimally or in moderation, and avoid for at least four hours before bedtime.

- Engage in relaxing activities before bed.

- Keep your bedroom calm, quiet, and cool.

- Avoid clock-watching at night, especially after going to bed.

- Exercise regularly, but not within two to four hours of bedtime.

- Avoid napping to minimize having trouble falling asleep at night.

Another common recommendation is to use the bed and bedroom only for sleeping and sexual activity. I also encourage removing as many electronics as possible from the bedroom, especially televisions, computers, and even smart phones if one is tempted to use them to check e-mail and send text messages when one is supposed to be sleeping.[13]

Some elephants are creatures in our rooms and in our lives that are so much a part of us and our routines that it does not even occur to us that they exist, let alone if they are tamed or wild. Sleep is such an elephant—we don't give it a thought when things are going well, but our quality of life, mood, energy, relationships, and even our ability to think and remember can suffer when this animal is out of control. The field of medicine is scrambling to get on top of this elephant, and strides are being made in the arena of public awareness of sleep issues. Of all of the elephants in the herd, this is definitely one pastors need to be on top of—not underfoot!

Remember, this chapter in no way substitutes for collaborative relationships with your physicians and dentist. Neither should it be used as an authoritative medical text or in the same way as one reads and files away patient education flyers you receive in your doctor's office. However, I hope it does reinforce the importance of regular medical care, that it is more than "just OK" to take care of yourself—it's essential to your ministry, your family, and yourself. The concerns mentioned in this chapter just happen to be a few particularly common ones in the ranks of clergy and religious professionals.

As must be obvious by now, I am convinced that good physical health not only synergizes our spiritual, emotional, and intellectual lives; it is essential to serving our Lord and the church, to thriving and excelling in the work we are called to do. Countless times I have reminded parents, family members, and friends of ill, even dying children, that often the best thing they can do for others is to take good care of themselves. This applies to pastors, too. Often, we confuse the effort and resources we might devote to good self-care with being selfish, inconsiderate, or a bad minister if we are not perpetually engaged in the pastoral care of our flock—even if the pastoral work suffers because we are unhealthy, tired, or burned out ourselves. Jesus instructed us to "love your neighbor *as yourself.*"[14] Caregivers, especially pastors, often operate as if taking responsible care of ourselves diminishes our love of neighbor or detracts from other things we might be doing for them. My experience caring for clergy as a psychiatrist and pastor has convinced me otherwise.

Do you remember my story about my colleague and me being misunderstood years ago when we suggested the church can model healthy living, particularly in the area of nutrition and fitness? I recently ran across our response, and think it even more relevant now today than when we first wrote it.

> The church too long has been silent on issues of physical health, despite biblical teaching that we are to be attentive to matters of the spirit, mind and body. We stated that the church is an untapped resource for teaching and modeling holy and healthy living. The silence of the corporate church has denied or minimized opportunities to support and care for individuals with [obesity] and other complex medical concerns. . . .

> We encourage the church to think more about self-care in all forms as stewardship of God's creation, to incorporate these concerns in teaching and practice, to be open to credible new information as it arises, but, above all, to be pastoral, nonjudgmental and loving to each other in this and all things.[15]

NOTES

Chapter One
Elephants

1. Eviatar Zerubavel, *The Elephant in the Room: Silence and Denial in Everyday Life* (New York: Oxford University Press, 2006), 11.

2. Christopher Chabris and Daniel Simons, *The Invisible Gorilla: And Other Ways Our Intuitions Deceive Us* (New York: Crown, 2010), 40-41. The book takes its title from a well-known experiment in which a gorilla appeared in a short film of two teams of people passing basketballs. One team had white shirts; the other team wore black. The game was videotaped and shown to volunteers. The instructions were to count the number of passes made by players wearing white. You can watch this video at www.theinvisiblegorilla.com; the video is about a minute long. Half of the volunteers in the original experiment were so focused on counting passes that they did not notice a student in a full-body gorilla suit walk onto the scene, thump her chest, and walk off the screen. This experiment demonstrated the *illusion of attention* as well as inattentional blindness (pp. 5-6).

3. "In only ten short years, 1979 to 1989, the elephant population was cut in half. The awesome possibility exists that they could become extinct in the coming century." (See Jean Brody, *Elephants: An Affectionate Portrait* (San Luis Obispo: Blake Publ., 1993), 41.

4. Zerubavel, *The Elephant in the Room*, 55.

5. Ibid., 53.

6. Ibid., 81.

7. Sara Gruen, *Water for Elephants* (New York: Workman Publishing, 2006).

8. Jeanne Stevenson-Moessner, "Re-arranging the Furniture: Feminist Values from Seminary to Parish," in *Feminist and Womanist Pastoral Theology*, eds. Bonnie Miller-McLemore and Brita Gill-Austern (Nashville: Abingdon Press, 1999).

9. Nelle Morton, *The Journey Is Home* (Beacon Press), 125, 127, 202-9.

Chapter Two
A Herd of Elephants

1. "News in Brief," *Telegraph Herald*, July 8, 2011, 3A.

2. Bruno G. Breitmeyer, *Blindspots: The Many Ways We Cannot See* (New York: Oxford University Press, 2010), 23.

3. Ibid., 22-23.

4. Charles Monroe Sheldon, *The Crucifixion of Philip Strong* (New York and London: Street and Smith, 1899), 7.

5. Ibid.

6. Ibid., 11.

7. Ibid., 132.

8. Ibid., 132-133.

9. Ibid., 133.

10. Barbara Brown Taylor, *Leaving Church: A Memoir of Faith* (New York: Harper, 2006), 26.

11. Ibid., 50.

12. Ibid., 37.

13. Ibid., 75.

14. Charles E. Hummel, *Tyranny of the Urgent!* (Downers Grove: InterVarsity Press, 1967, rev. ed. 1994), 5.

15. C. Carson, *The Autobiography of Martin Luther King* (New York: Warner, 2001), 1, as cited in Monica McGoldrick, Randy Gerson, and Sueli Petry, *Genograms: Assessment and Intervention* (New York & London: W.W. Norton & Co., 2008), 43.

16. Monica McGoldrick, Randy Gerson, and Sueli Petry, *Genograms: Assessment and Intervention* (New York & London: W.W. Norton & Co., 2008), 132.

17. Ibid.

18. Flannery O'Connor, *Wise Blood* (New York: Farrar, Straus and Giroux, 1949), 14.

19. Ibid., 16.

20. Ibid.

21. Ibid.

22. Kenneth C. Haugk, *Antagonists in the Church: How to Identify and Deal with Destructive Conflict* (Minneapolis: Augsburg, 1988), 72.

Chapter Three
Stampede (or, "You Have Destroyed Our Sweet Little Church")

1. Martin Hanford, *Where's Wally?* (Walker Books in the UK, 1987), was the original publication. Wally's name was changed to Waldo for the U.S.A. publications.

2. Delort, *The Life and Lore of the Elephant*, 29.

3. Jeffrey Moussaieff Masson and Susan McCarthy, *When Elephants Weep: The Emotional Lives of Animals* (New York: Bantam Doubleday Dell, 1995).

4. Ibid., 54-55.

5. Ibid., 55.

6. www.worldprayers.org, Rabbi Harold Kushner, "A Prayer for the World," 2003.

7. Marilyn Hirsh, *Hannibal and His 37 Elephants* (New York: Holiday House, 1977).

Chapter Four
The Elephant That Crushes Your Spirit: Depression

1. "Puff (The Magic Dragon)," words and music by Peter Yarrow and Leonard Lipton, 1963.

2. O. Gonzalez, J. T. Berry, L. R. McKnight-Eily, T. Strine, V. J. Edwards, H. Lu, and J. B. Croft, "Current depression among adults— United States, 2006 and 2008," *Centers for Disease Control and Prevention Morbidity and Mortality Weekly Report* 59, No. 38 (2010): 1229-35.

3. All names and references are used as illustrations only and are drawn from multiple cases. All names are fictional, and any resemblance to actual persons is strictly coincidental.

4. Philippians 4:4 and Galatians 5:22-23 (NRSV).

5. American Psychiatric Association, *Diagnostic and Statistical Manual of Mental Disorders, Fourth Edition, Text Revision.* (Washington, D.C.: American Psychiatric Association, 2000).

6. Ibid., 45-428.

7. J. A. Joska and D. J. Stein, "Mood Disorders," in *The American Psychiatric Publishing Textbook of Psychiatry*, 5th ed., eds. E. Hales, S.

C. Yudofsky, and G. O. Gabbard (Washington, D.C.: American Psychiatric Publishing, Inc., 2008), 457-503.

8. Ibid.

9. American Psychiatric Association, *Practice Guideline for the Treatment of Patients with Major Depressive Disorder,* 3rd ed. (2010). Available at http://psychiatryonline.org, accessed on May 16, 2012.

10. APA, *Practice Guideline;* Joska and Stein, "Mood Disorders."

11. By this I mean that seniors will complain about depression if enough people tell them they are depressed or if they think they are supposed to be depressed (or in some cases, if it elicits attention from family or friends!). Seniors are much less likely than are younger people to volunteer that they are depressed or to start complaining about their depressive symptoms without being asked or prompted.

12. D. G. Blazer, "Treatment of Seniors," in *The American Psychiatric Publishing Textbook of Psychiatry,* 5th ed., eds. E. Hales, S. C. Yudofsky, and G. O. Gabbard (Washington, D.C.: American Psychiatric Publishing, Inc., 2008), 1449-69.

13. V. K. Purt and K. Stein, "Treatment of Women," in *The American Psychiatric Publishing Textbook of Psychiatry,* 5th ed., eds. E. Hales, S. C. Yudofsky, and G. O. Gabbard (Washington, D.C.: American Psychiatric Publishing, Inc., 2008), 1489-1525.

14. S. V. Cochran and F. E. Rabinowitz, *Men and Depression: Clinical and Empirical Perspectives* (San Diego: Academic Press, 2000); W. Pollack, "Mourning, Melancholia and Masculinity: Recognizing and Treating Depression in Men," in *New Psychotherapy for Men,* eds. W. Pollack and R. Levant (New York: Wiley, 1998), 147-166.

15. APA, *Practice Guideline.*

16. M. Li and G. Rodin, "Depression," in *The American Psychiatric Publishing Textbook of Psychosomatic Medicine,* 2nd ed., ed. J. L. Levenson (Washington, D.C.: American Psychiatric Publishing, Inc., 2011), 175-197.

17. APA, *Practice Guideline;* M. Martinez, L. B. Marangell, and J. M. Martinez, "Psychopharmacology," in *The American Psychiatric Publishing Textbook of Psychosomatic Medicine,* 2nd ed., ed. J. L. Levenson (Washington, D.C.: American Psychiatric Publishing, Inc., 2011), 1053-1131.

18. R. Temple, "Anti-depressant use in pediatric populations," FDA, accessed October 26, 2011. Available at: www.fda.gov/NewsEvents/Testimony/ucm113265.htm.

19. T. A. Hammad, T. Laughren, and J. Racoosin, "Suicidality in Pediatric Patients Treated with Antidepressant Drugs," *Archives of General Psychiatry* 64 (2007): 466-72.

20. M. Stone, T. Laughren, M. L. Jones, et al., "Risk of Suicidality in Clinical Trials of Antidepressants in Adults: Analysis of Proprietary Data Submitted for U.S. Food and Drug Administration," *BMJ* 339 (2009): b2880.

21. R. D. Gibbons, C. H. Brown, K. Hur, et al., "Early Evidence on the Effects of Regulators' Suicidality Warnings on SSRI Prescriptions and Suicides in Children and Adolescents," *American Journal of Psychiatry* 164 (2007): 1356-63; A. M. Libby, H. D. Orton, and R. J. Valuck, "Persisting Decline in Treatment of Pediatric Depression after FDA Warnings," *Archives of General Psychiatry* 66 (2009): 1122-24.

22. J. D. Hamilton and J. Bridge, "Supportive Psychotherapy, SSRIs, and MDD," *Journal of the American Academy of Child and Adolescent Psychiatry* 45 (2006): 6-7.

23. APA, *Practice Guideline.*

24. APA, *Practice Guideline*; M. S. George, Z. H. Nahas, J. J. Borckardt, B. Anderson, and M. J. Foust, Jr., "Nonpharmacological Somatic Treatments," in *The American Psychiatric Publishing Textbook of Psychosomatic Medicine,* 2nd ed., ed. J. L. Levenson (Washington, D.C.: American Psychiatric Publishing, Inc., 2011), 1133-53; Joska and Stein, "Mood Disorders."

25. The National Institute of Mental Health, "Suicide in the U.S.: Statistics and Prevention" (2010), accessed on August 23, 2012, http://

www.nimh.nih.gov/health/publications/suicide-in-the-us-statistics-and-prevention/index.shtml/.

26. APA, *Practice Guideline.*

27. The National Institute of Mental Health, "Suicide in the U.S."

28. American Board of Psychiatry and Neurology, Inc., accessed on August 24, 2012, http://www.abpn.com/.

29. American Psychological Association, accessed August 24, 2012, http://www.apa.org/about/index.aspx..

30. National Association of Social Workers, accessed August 24, 2012, http://www.naswdc.org.

31. American Association of Pastoral Counselors, accessed October 2, 2011, http://aapc.org..

32. "AAMFT," American Association for Marriage and Family Therapy, accessed October 2, 2011, http://www.aamft.org/iMIS15/AAMFT/.

33. The National Institute of Mental Health, "Suicide in the U.S."

Chapter Five
Wild Elephants That Trample and Crush: A.k.a.
"Dealing with Problematic Parishioners"

1. All names and references are used as illustrations only and are drawn from multiple cases. All names are fictional, and any resemblance to actual persons is strictly coincidental.

2. G. S. Truant and J. G. Lohrenz, "Basic Principles of Psychotherapy II: The Patient Model, Interventions, and Countertransference," *American Journal of Psychotherapy* 47 (1993): 19-32; R. J. Ursano, S. M. Sonnenberg, and S. G. Lazar, "Psychodynamic Psychotherapy," in *The American Psychiatric Publishing Textbook of Psychiatry*, 5th ed., eds. R. E. Hales, S. C. Yudofsky, and G. O. Gabbard, accessed September 1, 2012, http://psychiatryonline.org/content.aspx?bookid=3&section id=1347157.

3. D. A. Misch, "Basic Strategies of Dynamic Supportive Therapy," *Journal of Psychotherapy Practice and Research* 9 (2000): 173-89.

4. R. M. Lijtmaer, "The Patient Who Believes and the Analyst Who Does Not," *Journal of the American Academy of Psychoanalysis and Dynamic Psychiatry* 37 (2009): 99-110.

5. J. Kay, "The Essentials of Psychodynamic Psychotherapy," *Focus* 4 (2006): 167-72; Misch, "Basic Strategies"; Ursano, Sonnenberg, and Lazar, "Psychodynamic Psychotherapy."

6. J. J. Kreisman and H. Straus, *I Hate You—Don't Leave Me: Understanding the Borderline Personality* (New York: Avon Books, 1989); Kay, "The Essentials of Psychodynamic Psychotherapy"; and Ursano, Sonnenberg, and Lazar, "Psychodynamic Psychotherapy."

7. G. O. Gabbard, "Psychodynamic Approaches to Personality Disorders," *Focus* 3 (2005): 363-67; J. M. Oldham, "Personality Disorders," *Focus* 3 (2005): 372-82; A. E. Skodol and J. G. Gunderson, "Personality Disorders," in *The American Psychiatric Publishing Textbook of Psychiatry* 5th ed., eds. R. E. Hales, S. C. Yudofsky, and G. O. Gabbard (2008), accessed September 1, 2012, http://psychiatryonline.org/content.aspx?bookid=3&sectionid=1341844.

8. Readers interested in a historical overview of the diagnostic and treatment approaches to personality disorders, including views of the different schools of psychological theory, will appreciate Dr. John Oldham's review article on personality disorders referenced in the footnote above.

9. American Psychiatric Association, *Diagnostic and Statistical Manual, Fourth Edition, Text Revision.* (Washington, D.C.: American Psychiatric Association, 2000).

10. M. Zimmerman, L. Rothschild, and I. Chelminski, "The Prevalence of DSM-IV Personality Disorders in Psychiatric Outpatients," *American Journal of Psychiatry* 162 (2005): 1911-18.

11. S. Torgersen, "Epidemiology," in *The American Psychiatric Publishing Textbook of Personality Disorders*, eds. J. M. Oldham, A. E.

Skodol, and D. S. Bender (Washington, D.C.: American Psychiatric Publishing, 2005), 129-41.

12. Skodol and Gunderson, "Personality Disorders."

13. American Psychiatric Association, *DSM-IV-TR*.

14. In the psychiatric literature, Glen Gabbard, MD, and Thomas Gutheil, MD, are acknowledged to be leading experts on healthy therapist boundaries, boundary crossings, and boundary violations. They have written extensively on the subject. One important paper for psychiatrists on this issue is T. G. Gutheil and G. O. Gabbard, "Misuses and Misunderstandings of Boundary Theory in Clinical and Regulatory Settings," *American Journal of Psychiatry* 155 (1998): 409-14.

Chapter Six
And the Elephant in the Room Is . . . the Preacher!

1. J. Guirguis-Blake, T. Wolff, R. Crichlow, J. E. Wilson, and D. Meyers, "Preventive Health Care," in *Textbook of Family Medicine*, 8th ed., eds. R. E. Rakel and D. P. Rakel (Philadelphia: Saunders, 2011), 73-99; C. P. Kopes-Kerr, "Lifestyle Interventions and Behavior Change," in *Textbook of Family Medicine*, 8th ed., eds. R. E. Rakel and D. P. Rakel (Philadelphia: Saunders, 2011), 100-111.

2. Ibid.

3. The American College of Obstetricians and Gynecologists (ACOG), "Weight Control: Eating Right and Keeping Fit (FAQ064)," accessed August 1, 2012, http://www.acog.org/For_Patients/Patient_Education_FAQs_List. American College of Physicians (ACP), "Overweight/Obesity and Weight Control," accessed August 8, 2012, http://www.acponline.org/patients_families/diseases_conditions/obesity/.

4. ACP, "Overweight/Obesity and Weight Control."

5. National Institute of Diabetes and Digestive and Kidney Diseases (NIDDK) Weight-control Information Network (WIN), "Getting on Track: Physical Activity and Healthy Eating for Men," accessed August 23, 2012, http://win.niddk.nih.gov/publications/gettingontrack.htm; The American College of Obstetricians and Gynecologists

(ACOG), "Exercise and Fitness (FAQ045)," accessed on August 1, 2012, http://www.acog.org/For_Patients/Patient_Education_FAQs_ List.

6. National Institutes of Health, "NIH New in Health," October 2009, accessed August 10, 2012, http://newsinhealth.nih.gov/2009/ October.

7. All names and references are used as illustrations only and are drawn from multiple cases. All names are fictional, and any resemblance to actual persons is strictly coincidental.

8. U.S. Preventive Services Task Force (USPSTF), "The Guide to Clinical Preventive Services 2010-2011," accessed August 1, 2012, http://www.ahrq.gov/clinic/pocketgd.htm.

9. Guirguis-Blake et al., "Preventive Health Care."

10. L. A. Panossian and A. Y. Avidan, "Review of Sleep Disorders," *Medical Clinics of North America* 93 (2009): 407-25.

11. American Psychiatric Association, *Diagnostic and Statistical Manual of Mental Disorders, Fourth Edition, Text Revision.* (Washington, D.C.: The American Psychiatric Association), 2000, 597-661; D. J. Buysse, P. J. Strollo, Jr., J. E. Black, P. G. Zee, and J. W. Winkelman. "Sleep Disorders," in: R. E. Hales, S. C. Yudofsky, and G. O. Gabbard, editors. *The American Psychiatric Textbook of Psychiatry,* 5th ed., (Washington, D.C.: American Psychiatric Publishing, 2008), 921-69.

12. Ibid.

13. R. M. Benca, "Diagnosis and Treatment of Chronic Insomnia: A Review," *Psychiatric Services* 56 (2005): 332-43; E. J. Stepanski and J. K. Wyatt, "Use of Sleep Hygiene in the Treatment of Insomnia," *Sleep Medicine Reviews* 7 (2003): 215-25.

14. Matthew 19:19 (NRSV).

15. M. L. Dell and A. T. P. Merrow, "Church Silent Too Long," *Episcopal Life*, March 2004, vol. 15, no. 3, 24.

250
M694

127780

CPSIA information can be obtained at www.ICGtesting.com
Printed in the USA
LVOW080710140513

333583LV00002B

3 4711 00218 4291

9 781426 753213